THE
TACTICAL
SHOTGUN

Dedicated to my friend and mentor Colonel Jeff Cooper— USMCR—a gentleman, a warrior, a patriot, and a philosopher. The world will not see his like again. *Viva el Coronel!*

THE
TACTICAL
SHOTGUN

**The Best Techniques and Tactics for
Employing the Shotgun in Personal Combat**

Gabriel Suarez

Paladin Press · Boulder, Colorado

*The Tactical Shotgun: The Best Techniques and Tactics for
    Employing the Shotgun in Personal Combat*
by Gabriel Suarez

Copyright © 1996 Gabriel Suarez

ISBN 0-87364-898-6
Printed in the United States of America

Published by Paladin Press, a division of
Paladin Enterprises, Inc., P.O. Box 1307,
Boulder, Colorado 80306, USA.
(303) 443-7250

Direct inquiries and/or orders to the above address.

PALADIN, PALADIN PRESS, and the "horse head" design
are trademarks belonging to Paladin Enterprises and
registered in United States Patent and Trademark Office.

TABLE OF CONTENTS

ACKNOWLEDGEMENTS

*"Think where man's glory
most begins and ends,
And say my glory was I had
such friends."*

—William Butler Yeats,
The Spur

As usual, the list is long. Most of all, I want to thank Colonel Jeff Cooper for reviewing the manuscript and helping to sort it out. I will always be indebted for his training in attitude development and mind-set, which seem to keep saving my hide.

Thanks also to my wife and best friend, Cheryl Suarez (the tactical photographer), who endured and enhanced the making of a second book.

Thanks to Dr. Ignatius Piazza and the warriors at the Front Sight Firearms Training Institute. Top-shelf people, every one of them.

Thanks to Officers Richard

Camacho and Eric Uyeno of the Santa Monica Police Department Spec-Ops Division/Crime Impact Team for their assistance with the photographs.

And last, but not least, to the people at Paladin Press who helped get this project "squared away." You tell the truth, even when the truth is not popular.

FOREWORD

As the founder and director of Front Sight Firearms Training Institute and the second man in the world to secure a Four Weapons Combat Master certificate, I believe I am qualified to state that of the four weapons, the shotgun is by far the most elementary. Any beginning student of weaponcraft will notice immediately that the task of placing a quick, decisive hit on one's adversary, within the ranges most often encountered in gunfights, is much easier with a shotgun, as compared to the handgun, rifle, or submachine gun. In fact, at Front Sight Firearms

Training Institute, we routinely take uninitiated, tactical shotgun students and intensively train them to a distinguished level of competence in a remarkably short period of time.

With the ease in which students of weaponcraft become proficient in the use of the tactical shotgun, one may wonder why another textbook devoted to the shotgun is necessary at all. Others have already written books on the subject. The gun journals rehash old shotgun articles every year, and the shotgun has not really changed considerably since its inception. So why read this book, *The Tactical Shotgun*? You will find your answer, as I did, in the essence of this exceptional work.

Any of today's "experts" can write a manual outlining the proper procedures and techniques employed in the use of weapons. With slight variations, the procedures all have reasonably good results as long as the authors have a workable understanding of weapon manipulation, sight picture, sight alignment, and trigger control. However, weapon handling and marksmanship are just a part of the equation. When pressed to reveal the combat experience that founded their respective conclusions, only a few authors can state that they have repeatedly stared into the face of death—sneered—and delivered the lead bouquet. Gabriel Suarez is one the few. No doubt about it: Gabriel Suarez is the quintessential warrior.

Intertwined with every shotgun technique and tactic covered in this test, you will find the fighting spirit of a man who holds the combat mind-set and skill at arms in reverence while granting the enemy nothing but contempt. It is this fighting spirit, combined with the combat-proven tactics outlined herein, that separates the victorious from the dead in our urban battle zones. It is this fighting spirit and tactical awareness that you must understand and adopt for yourself, if you hope to stand tall when the chips are down. Gabriel Suarez has given you what many authors are simply unable to give: the truth about winning a gunfight.

For those who seek their knowledge only from those who truly know, *The Tactical Shotgun* and its companion, *The Tactical Pistol*, are required reading. Study them well!

—Ignatius Piazza

INTRODUCTION

*"To count the life of battle good
And dear the land that gave you birth,
And dearer yet the brotherhood
That binds the brave of all the earth."*
—Sir Henry Newbolt,
*The Island Race,
Clifton Chapel*

The basic concept of the shotgun has been in existence since Leonardo da Vinci started fingerpainting way back in the 15th century. You can well imagine how some embattled musketeer might have easily been tempted to load his smoothbore with a handful of whatever instead of the prescribed single ball in order to create more devastating wounds and, who knows, maybe even get two with one shot.

The historical path of the scattergun actually parallels that of other shoulder-fired arms. Its dual roles as a food-gathering tool for the hunter

1

and an antipersonnel weapon for the warrior developed concurrently.

Until recently, the shotgun was considered too brutal by most European countries and was largely abandoned as a combat tool. (Just not cricket, old boy.) However, the shotgun is still a classic American fighting tool. Historically, it has seen action in every major military conflict involving U.S. forces.

From the time when General Washington admonished his troops to load with "buck and ball" to its use during the war with Mexico and the War Between the States to the many "difficulties" in the Old West—the shotgun remained the choice of many professionals who went in harm's way. It went "over there" with our boys in the form of trench guns during the first "war to end all wars." The U.S. shotgun was there again during round two in the Pacific and European theaters, not to mention the many wars for liberation and independence and assorted police actions into the present day.

In its civilian role, the shotgun has managed to stay accessible in even the most tyrannically gun-restrictive jurisdictions. This socially acceptable, if not politically correct, status makes it a natural choice for urban home and business protection by a private citizen. Also, in our age of kinder-gentler, politically oriented policing, the shotgun's inoffensive visage guarantees its place as the street cop's silent partner for those "business meetings" requiring more insurance than a pistol can provide.

Such widespread acceptance has guaranteed the shotgun's future in the tactical scheme of things, but it has also given rise to all sorts of misconceptions about its true role and purpose. The shotgun is a specialized tool that, in its tactical role, serves its user like no other weapon can. Many well-meaning tacticians, however, have tried to make the shotgun into a versatile all-things-for-all-gunfighters weapon. This is a grave mistake. There are no really versatile weapons, because each

2

The shotgun has been the policeman's silent partner for those "business meetings" requiring more than just a pistol.

3

type was designed for a particular purpose. So it is with the combat shotgun.

The shotgun is best suited for close-range, short-duration conflicts that do not require a great deal of firepower (i.e., rounds per target) or extreme penetration. The forgiving nature of its ammunition makes the shotgun particularly useful for low-light encounters or situations where the antagonists are moving quickly. Additionally, it is an easy weapon to learn, and its manual of arms is uncomplicated.

If the shotgun is used within these stated limits, its unique characteristics can be invaluable in accomplishing the mission. But if these characteristics are ignored, the results may be devastating. For example, the shotgun's quickly spreading buckshot pattern would be an asset for dealing with multiple hostiles in a darkened urban environment, but a sore liability if used for a hostage-rescue situation. Its low-penetration characteristics are a boon when dealing with home or business defense, but bad news if you require a shot at an adversary ensconced behind hard cover. Likewise, its short range endears it to those dealing with trouble in congested urban areas in the event of a miss (horrors!), but this same characteristic is deadly if the weapon is chosen to deal with a rifleman at 200 paces!

A well-trained shotgunner *might* be able to overcome all these obstacles, but if these problems are perceived before the fact, selecting a more suitable weapon is preferable to making do with an inappropriate tool when the shooting starts.

The nature of the shotgun defines the situations in which it will likely be used, which amazingly parallel those normally involving the pistol. A broad mission statement for the shotgun might be the following: "A shotgun is what you take to an immediately *expected* pistol fight."

The greatest failing of the shotgun has been the training of the combat shotgunner (or more accurately, the lack of training). This training, usually conducted by an old bird hunter with no combat experience, would typically consist of an explanation why the shotgun is always pointed "instinctively" and never aimed, followed by a few sessions of clay bird busting. Once adept at trap and skeet, the fledgling master blaster would be sent out into the world . . . officially certified as *combat ready!*

The problem with this concept is that the combat use of the shotgun has as much in common with its sporting use as hand-to-hand combat has with pro wrestling. Even in today's tactically advanced training environment, the shotgun is still quite often misunderstood, mismanaged, and misused.

Additionally, proficiency with the tool itself is only part of the package. Training the mind and cultivating the right attitudes are equally important. The shotgun is a fighting tool with which we may be required to kill another person. The idea of being shot at and then shooting back in anger is alien to many of us. But if you spend the better part of 10 years living in one of the most dangerous places in America, as I have, you'll discover that you never step out of the old hacienda without that little thought in the back of your mind . . . "maybe tonight." If you do not want to be a statistic, dear reader, you must do likewise.

The objective of this, my second book, is to examine the tactical shotgun's true role in personal combat and illustrate the best methods of employing it against human adversaries at the moment of truth. There are some tactical concepts I will point out that were described in *The Tactical Pistol*, my previous book, and which will not be repeated here. Keep in mind, though, that those concepts are just as applicable to the scattergun as they are to the one-handed gun.

My experience with the shotgun is not minor by anyone's standards. I have carried it in the real world and looked at the "elephant" over its sights several times. If a human being is capable of manifesting affection for an inanimate object, then there will always be a special place in my heart for the shotgun. I reserve that right for myself because without an understanding of the shotgun and its very presence in my hands, I might have perished long ago on a cold December night outside of a convenience store during a disagreement with three armed robbers. The lack of such an understanding may very well have contributed to the untimely death of many good people (both in and out of uniform) . . . some of whom were my friends.

Although tactical knowledge and skill at arms cannot ensure success in a gunfight (since such social functions carry no guarantees), they may provide that very fine edge that separates victory and defeat. This very edge might have kept a street cop's eyes open long enough to see one more sunrise . . . and might have permanently closed those of the criminal that killed him instead! So study this volume, digest it, sharpen your edge, and get friendly with *The Tactical Shotgun*.

Gabriel Suarez
Los Angeles, 1996

CHAPTER ONE

SAFETY CONCERNS

"There are no such things as dangerous weapons. There are only dangerous men."

—Robert Heinlein,
Methuselah's Children

No book on tactical shooting (with any weapon) should commence without a discussion of safety. The bottom line about firearms is that they are *all* dangerous. That is how they were intended to be. If they were not, they would be useless. But in reality, it is not the tool that is dangerous, but the careless user of such tools. Safety with guns, like safety with cars or chainsaws, demands a certain degree of common sense. Perhaps this in itself is wishful thinking in a time when such sense is not as "common" as it once was. To augment common sense, there are four safe-

7

Safety with weapons is a matter of concentration.

ty rules—simple and applicable in any environment—
that an operator must observe while handling weapons.

1. *All guns are always loaded.* People are
   automatically more careful with a gun they know is
   loaded, just as they are more careful with a knife
   they know is sharp. Furthermore, because an empty
   gun would be useless, you should just assume that
   any gun you encounter is loaded. Whenever you are
   handed a firearm, or pick one up for examination,
   inspect it and, if necessary, unload it.
2. *Never let the muzzle cover anything (or anyone)
   that you are not willing to destroy.* This rule is
   applicable in administrative handling as well as in
   tactical situations. If someone points a shotgun (or
   any weapon) at you, you are quite justified in taking
   it harshly since you can reasonably infer that he is
   willing to destroy you. The excuse usually heard
   through the gun wielder's newly swelling lips and
   bleeding gums is, "But it wasn't loaded." Your
   response should be, "See rule one!"
       When handling tactical problems, you do

8

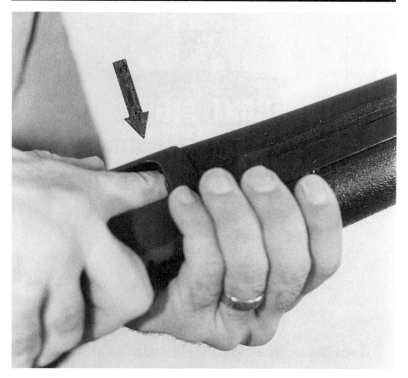

All guns are always loaded. A shotgun is checked visually and by touch by inserting a finger into the chamber, as illustrated here.

sometimes cover presumed hostiles with your muzzle. Doing so is not a violation of this rule because if you perceive that someone is an enemy, you sure as @#&* better be willing to destroy him before he does it to you first. If it turns out that no shooting is required, then simply lower the muzzle and request an explanation of his activities. You can avoid this problem by observing rule number three.

3. *Keep your finger off the trigger until your sights are on the target.* In the tactical situation discussed above, your sights were not on the target yet . . . or at least you weren't looking at them. You were still

9

1. Every gun is always loaded.
2. Never let the muzzle cover anything you are not willing to destroy.
3. Keep your finger off the trigger until your sights are on the target.
4. Always be sure of your target.

The four rules of gun safety as instituted by Jeff Cooper and taught at Front Sight.

looking at the possible threat. Excluding body contact or weapon-retention shots, if you haven't picked up your sight picture, you do not touch the trigger. This final safeguard prevents unintentional shots. At all times, even when moving "on the hunt," looking for a target, keep trigger fingers off the trigger until it is necessary to shoot.

4. *Be sure of your target and what is beyond it.* Do not shoot at sounds or shadows because they might not be what you think. Indiscriminately shooting at noises is embarrassing and often causes tragedies, and every such tragedy is used as fodder by the gun-control activists among us to foist antigun laws on us and further corrupt our liberty. Don't let this happen to you—be sure of your target! Additionally, be aware of what is behind and around that criminal you are about to smite.

This is not only a consideration if overpenetration occurs, but also in cases of missed shots (it happens to all of us). A discussion of methods to prevent such hazards if shots must still be fired is presented later—learn them!

Notice that these rules are not based on weapons hardware, but rather on the software between your ears—your own mind-set. They are applicable for life, and you must always observe them when handling firearms.

CHAPTER TWO

AMMUNITION
THE HEART OF THE FIGHTING SHOTGUN

"Wars may be fought with weapons, but they are won by men."
—General George S. Patton, U.S. Army, in the *Cavalry Journal* (September 1933)

Although the shotgun can launch a variety of projectiles, including birdshot, buckshot, slugs, and specialty munitions, it is unlikely that the shotgunner will have such a considerable array of choices at his disposal, much less the time to make the switch—particularly if the shotgun is used in a reactive environment. Reality tells us that what the shotgun is loaded with at the beginning of the fight will likely be the type of ammo used to (it is hoped) win that fight.

When the shotgun is selected specifically for antipersonnel use, the variety of ammunition choices decreas-

The shotgun is different than other small arms because of its ammunition.

es markedly. In such cases, we are limited to birdshot, buckshot, and slugs. I've purposely omitted tactical specialty loads such as tear gas, door breaching, and others because they are designed for purposes other than shooting humans. They will be discussed later. Keep in mind that the ammunition type selected for the shotgun more than anything else dictates its mission.

Birdshot, for example, would be a foolish choice for anything but a strict home-defense application, where engagement distances will be remarkably close, and overpenetration is a major concern. This is the only place where tactical use of birdshot is worthwhile. Buckshot will easily penetrate walls and sometimes even sail right through an adversary's body (I have seen this on two occasions). With birdshot, you will have ample stopping power with reduced risks if you miss the adversary with a couple of pellets. Even if you pull the entire charge of birdshot off target, it will be absorbed by the double Sheetrock wall. Yes, some pellets might make it through, but the physical damage to uninvolved personnel will be inconsequential compared to what buckshot would have done. The best choices here are the #7 1/2 or #8 low-base, 7/8-ounce loads. Selecting the more powerful versions of trap-skeet loads is not a good idea because they will have greater penetration without any real stopping power benefits over the #7 1/2 or #8 loads. Within room combat distances, #7 1/2 and #8 birdshot will strike an adversary as a single mass and generally will not overpenetrate.

The same characteristics that make birdshot the best thing since sliced bread for home defense make it a poor choice for general-purpose deployment. Anytime you take the shotgun out of the house, replace the birdshot with buckshot.

Buckshot is largely responsible for the shotgun's reputation as a fight stopper. Buckshot can give you riflelike power and close-quarters performance without the danger of extended range or overpenetration, which makes the use of the rifle so risky in congested urban environments. It is important to know that buckshot patterns tend to spread out in a conical format as the shot column leaves the barrel and proceeds downrange. The amount of pattern dispersal depends on the type of buckshot used as well as the individual characteristics of the shotgun barrel. Very few shotguns will "pattern" alike with various ammunition brands. This necessitates thorough experimentation with different brands and shot sizes. The best efficiency is obtained by keeping the shot charge together as far as possible, not in spreading it out, as was previously believed (the old "alley broom" concept).

Advancements in buckshot design have given us the plastic shot collar, or cup, to reduce the deformation of the pellets as they contact the bore walls on the way out.

The addition of granulated polymer fillers further protect the pellets against the forces encountered during the internal ballistics phase. More recently, hardened and copper-plated premium and "tactical" buckshot has further enhanced this load's boarder-repelling qualities. The most prevalent of these is Federal's H132 Tactical Load of nine-pellet 00-Buck (velocity is 1,150 feet per second (fps)—standard buckshot travels at 1,300 fps). This load has a reduced powder charge of faster burning powder and exhibits reduced recoil yet tighter patterns and slightly less penetration. I recommend Tactical Load for smaller shooters who've experienced problems handling or controlling their shotguns.

Don't make the mistake of thinking that because buckshot holds nine .36-caliber pellets, it is the equivalent of nine simultaneous pistol shots. A buckshot pellet is not the equivalent of a pistol bullet even if the caliber is the same. The ballistically poor shape of individual pellets cause them to lose much of their velocity as well as penetration potential by the time they reach the 40-yard line. Even at 25 yards, their velocity and penetration ability has diminished by about one-half. This is still a close-range tool.

Buckshot achieves its stopping-power effectiveness by virtue of multiple, simultaneous hits, which increase the quantity of injury and shock effect that a single pistol bullet (or buckshot pellet) cannot match (more on this later).

When selecting a load for your particular weapon, you must remember that the larger buckshot loads containing fewer pellets (#000, #00, #0) often exhibit rapidly deteriorating pattern density as the range increases. Conversely, the smaller shot sizes (#1 and #4) may provide better pattern density but at the cost of decreased penetration of the target. Choose your ammo carefully, based on your perceived needs.

The third type of antipersonnel ammo is the rifled

slug. This load turns the shotgun into a sort of makeshift short-range rifle. Some authorities suggest exclusive use of rifled slugs and eschew buckshot completely. I disagree: if you do that, you no longer have a shotgun, but rather a rifle. If you want to solve what are obvious long-distance conflicts, just use a rifle in the first place, no? The exclusive use of slugs negates the shotgun's main advantage—that being the spreading shot pattern that allows imprecise aiming and subsequently greater speed in close-range scuffles. Rifled slugs are in reality specialty rounds that you bring along in case the typical close-range fight goes beyond the extreme maximum distance of the buckshot load.

A rifle-sighted shotgun with a high-quality slug can allow an operator to hit targets out to 100 yards. The rifled slug is available in three basic formats: the U.S. Foster-type slug, the German Brenneke, and various sabot types. All three versions use different designs in an attempt to stabilize the slug by making it heavier at the front end. The intent is to make the slug act like a badminton shuttlecock.

The U.S. Foster-type slugs are actually a thick cup of lead weighing about 1 ounce. The nose of these slugs is usually rounded, although one U.S. company is now making them in a "Hydra-shok" hollowpoint configuration. The looks of a Foster slug resemble an inverted shot glass. Brenneke slugs are also nose heavy and cylindrical. The difference is in the short pointed tip and in the Phillips screw-affixed wadding of the Brenneke. Brennekes are reputed to penetrate substantially deeper than most other types. Many northern woodsmen, in fact, favor a Brenneke-loaded shotgun for close-range emergency anti-bear duty. The sabot slug is a .50-caliber (instead of .72 as are the Foster and Brenneke), hour-glass-shaped bullet encased in a pair of plastic sabots that together fit the internal dimensions of the shotgun bore. The plastic sabots drop off quickly after firing, allowing the ballistically superior "bullet" to travel toward the target more accurately. Additionally, since the slug does not touch the internal barrel walls directly, it can be made of a harder alloy than is common with the other two types.

Each type of ammunition is designed for a specific function, and the wise shotgunner can match munitions with mission.

CHAPTER THREE

PATTERNING TESTS
GETTING TO KNOW YOUR SHOTGUN

"If you know your enemy, and you know yourself, there will be no danger in 1,000 battles."

—Sun Tzu,
The Art of War

One of the rules of combat shotgunning is to *know your ammunition—and know your gun.* Knowing the patterning characteristics of your particular shotgun-ammunition combination allows you to determine if a particular shot is within your capabilities, or if refraining from taking the shot would be wiser.

When you begin to experiment with the shotgun and various brands of ammunition, you'll find that the degree of pattern dispersion may be divided roughly into three zones: A, B, and C.

19

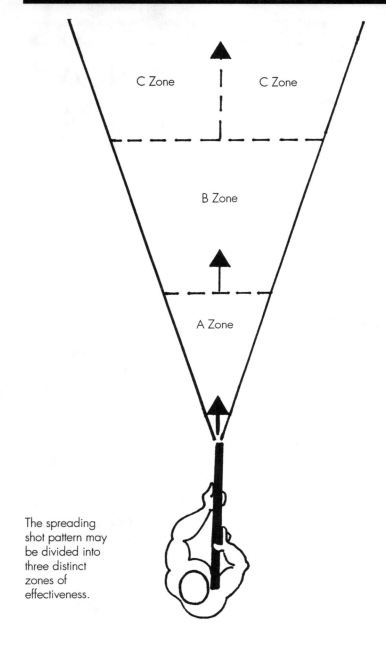

C Zone | C Zone

B Zone

A Zone

The spreading shot pattern may be divided into three distinct zones of effectiveness.

ZONES

A Zone

The A Zone generally extends from arm's length to seven paces. At this distance, the shot pattern has not had enough flight time to expand to any discernible degree, and its strike can be covered by a hand. In this zone you may as well be shooting a rifle bullet because that is exactly what the shot column behaves like. The stopping power of the shotgun at these how-do-you-do distances, with any sort of ammunition, is truly decisive.

Accurately placing the still condensed shot pattern on target is facilitated by using the weapon's sights. An alternate method for extremely close-range reactive shooting is to index the shotgun on target by using the underarm assault position. Note that this is *not* "instinctive shooting."

B Zone

When the engagement distances extend beyond 7 yards, you enter the distance wherein the conventional use of the shotgun can be exploited, the B Zone. Here, the pattern has had time to expand to the point where you may use the spread to distribute the blow and maximize the damage. Effective use in this zone can only be accomplished by using the weapon's sights. The expanding pattern allows you to engage and shoot very quickly—much more so than if you were using a single-projectile weapon. The limit of the B Zone will be reached when the pattern has expanded so much that a human adversary might be able to walk right through it unscathed! That point is usually reached at 20 to 25 yards, depending on the particular shotgun and ammunition in use.

Any shotgun with any buckshot brand, however, will perform as needed within 10 yards. Because most shotgun fights occur well within this distance, an unfamiliar

21

shotgun with untested ammunition will do in a tight spot. It is only when distances reach beyond this that you might run into problems if you haven't thoroughly tested the chosen (or assigned) weapon.

C Zone

Using the shotgun beyond its B Zone capabilities is virtually impossible with *any* buckshot. This is the C Zone—the point at which buckshot is no longer useful in a particular shotgun—and it usually begins at 20 to 25 yards. This is the realm of the rifled slug. The slug allows you to reach out to 100 yards if necessary. It turns the shotgun into a short-range rifle. Using a shotgun for extended shots with slugs requires that sights be mounted on the weapon. An off-the-rack shotgun equipped with a bead front sight will do fine up close and out to the extremes of the B Zone, but not with slugs.

If a fight extends beyond the capability of the buckshot-loaded shotgun, an operator *might* have time to load a slug in order to reach the required distance. This is mostly a matter of practice and availability of the slugs in the first place. Training is also a factor, because unless the operator has conditioned himself to respond to a distant target by loading and firing a slug, he might not even *think* of it until it is too late. It is still a wise idea to keep some slugs handy if the only weapon on hand is a shotgun and things suddenly get distant.

I recommend patterning an individual shotgun with the birdshot or buckshot intended for defensive use (and to zero with the chosen slug type as well). However, ammunition should not be selected solely on its patterning characteristics. For example, #4 buck tends to pattern better than some larger sizes of buckshot, but it will not *stop* an adversary nearly as well. Therefore, all factors must be considered before any final selection is made. For many professionals, the ammunition will undoubtedly be chosen for them. Sometimes the issued ammunition will be

22

excellent, and other times it may not be. In the latter situations, you must *adapt* and *overcome*.

When you begin the patterning procedure, the erratic nature of shot patterns will become evident. Sometimes a relatively condensed pattern will exhibit one or two "flyers" that are distinctly separated from the other pellet strikes. At other times the pattern will be doughnut shaped with a "clean" center. Many minute variables in barrel design, choking, and ammunition production contribute to such patterns, and there is little that can be done to affect them.

The patterning process begins by firing one round of shot at 5, 7, 10, 12, 15, 20, and 25 yards. Initially, the shot pattern will exhibit a virtual singular strike exemplified by one ragged hole in the target. When the ragged hole in the target begins to expand to a more conventional pattern, exhibiting holes from individual pellets, you've reached the B Zone. Transition from the A Zone to B Zone is unavoidable. The greatest concern is in determining which ammunition type will allow relatively condensed patterns and for the greatest distance in the B Zone. In the B Zone, pattern the gun and ammunition at increasing distances until you find that the majority of the pattern is no longer on the target. This is where experimentation with different brands and sizes of buckshot must occur. If the ammunition brand or size initially tested does not yield satisfactory results, try a different one. The noted tactician Chuck Taylor advises that 85 percent or more of the shot charge must hit the vital zone of the target at the maximum range every time to be considered for real-world use.

With all the ammunition manufacturers and different buckshot sizes available, finding something suitable should not be a problem. Whatever buckshot type you finally decide on, you will reach a point where the pattern will have spread too much and an enemy might be able to step right through it without getting nicked. The important thing is to note exactly at what distance this occurs, because a few feet short of that distance marks the working limit of your buckshot-loaded shotgun and the end of the B Zone.

As earlier explained, any activity with the combat shotgun beyond the B Zone requires the use of slugs. The slug-equipped shotgun must be zeroed in just as a rifle is zeroed in. It is substantially easier to begin the zeroing process at closer distances to "get the shots on paper" and then fine-tune the zero at the longer distances. With this in mind, initially zero the shotgun at the end of the B Zone. After producing a decent group, move back to 50 yards and fine-tune the sight adjustments. Considering the "real" distances where shotguns will likely be used with slugs, 50 yards is a good point to zero. Some people I've worked with have zeroed at 75 yards and even 100 yards because they have a likely chance of distant encounters. Whatever final zero is selected, you should know where the shotgun will hit at 25, 50, 75, and 100 yards.

Slug selection is similar to buckshot selection. Group the shotgun at 25 yards with various types of slugs and then select the most accurate. Next, continue testing the shotgun with the chosen brand of slugs to check its performance at varying distances.

When all this experimentation is completed, you will have an excellent short-range fight stopper with buckshot and medium-range riflelike capabilities with slugs in the event that a close-quarters dispute becomes a midrange affair.

CHAPTER FOUR

STOPPING POWER OF THE SHOTGUN

"Never do your enemy a minor injury."

—Niccolo Machiavelli,
The Prince

One of the reasons for selecting the shotgun for close confrontations is its reputation for decisive stopping power. The term *stopping power* is tossed around in tactical discussions with such frequency that it makes the listener feel like he's at a Ping-Pong match. Various authors have written extensively on the subject and have proposed many theories and notions. The problem with this approach is that theories and notions are not much help to the poor street cop hiding outside a stop-and-rob with a shotgun, waiting for Dillinger and his boys to exit stage right!

25

Of all the small arms, the shotgun has the greatest likelihood of a one-shot stop. Here a Las Vegas SWAT officer executes the Dozier multiple-target drill.

I am no scientist or medical examiner, but I've seen many folks shot with various cartridges (including shotguns) and have come to the realistic conclusion that there are no guarantees in a gunfight—particularly with stopping power. The only thing we can really expect to do is stack the deck in our favor as much as we can—selecting a shotgun goes a long way in the stacking department.

Colonel Jeff Cooper told me that of the shotgun fights reported to him, few ever exceeded two shots and that the vast majority were settled with only one shot. My own research and experiences confirm this. Of all the small arms available in the tactical inventory, few equal the shotgun in terms of close-range power to end hostilities. Let's examine why that is.

In *The Tactical Pistol*, I surmised that there were three factors affecting the possibility of stopping an adversary as a result of gunfire. The first of these is *shot placement*. Clearly, if you don't hit your target somewhere he considers important, he will not be impressed with your efforts and will probably redouble his efforts to finish you off. Shot placement is a result of marksmanship, which is affected, in turn, by training and the ability to remain cool under pressure.

If you are so rattled by an attempt on your life that you lose your head and miss, the attack will continue—but your breathing may not. This happens to people every day with all sorts of weapons but most often with single-projectile weapons such as pistols or carbines. This seems to occur less often with a buckshot-loaded shotgun because of its rapidly spreading pattern in the middle distance. The probability of *hitting* is greatly enhanced with a shotgun. A buckshot-filled shotgun doesn't require the finite sight alignment of single-projectile weapons. This means that we can still manage to obtain hits with an extremely rough sight picture when the tempo of events is reaching the limit of your reaction time. The ability to use the pattern for distribution of the blow facilitates getting hits on the adversary. They may not be center hits, true, but initial peripheral hits often lead to centered hits.

The second factor for incapacitating an adversary is simply *the amount of damage done by the shot(s)*. The damage, or extent of injury, caused is dependent on how deeply the projectile(s) penetrates and what is actually struck. This performance depends on ammunition design and number of actual hits.

The shotgun provides as much tissue penetration as necessary without excess, but there is always a risk of overpenetration. I witnessed two incidents where buckshot pellets completely traversed and exited the adversaries' torsos! This deep penetration at close range, coupled with the massed number of pellets, multiplies the probability of damage. Multiple hits striking en masse have a much greater effect than the sum of all the pellets individually and seem to create a sort of sensory overload whereby the body shuts off because of the overwhelming damage.

The third factor to consider is *the adversary's mental state prior to being hit, as well as his psychological reaction to being hit.* We've all heard the horror stories of the poor police officer who, shot in the arm, convinced himself that he was going to die and therefore did. But there are also stories of psycho criminals absorbing more ordnance than an angry Cape buffalo on cocaine and still not falling down.

If there is any unalterable rule to stopping power it is that *there are no guarantees.* The human body can, if substantially motivated, take an incredible amount of punishment and still go on to accomplish the mission. The history of warfare is rife with such stories, from the Crusades to the war in Bosnia, of soldiers taking a remarkable pounding but persevering, in spite of what would appear to be unsurvivable wounds, to kill their counterparts.

Much of this reflects on the chemical effects of the body's reaction to extreme alarm. The more warning that the victim has that a fight to the death is around the corner, the more supercharged adrenaline gets pumped into his system, thus making him very difficult to stop. If you add alcohol, drugs, or fanaticism to the mix, the difficulty of stopping such an individual with minimum force increases dramatically.

Failures to stop with a shotgun are not as common as with pistols, but they still do occur. A basic study of physiology and wound mechanics will illustrate that there are two ways that gunshots (of any sort) incapacitate a human being. The first way (and easier in terms of target size) is to cause enough damage and bleeding so that blood pressure drops to a point where the adversary becomes unconscious. This is most easily done with a center-of-mass hit.

In pistolcraft, shooters generally try to place two or three hits in the chest (center of mass) first and proceed to the cranial shot if the prior shots have been ineffective. There are two reasons why we do this: 1) pistols are relatively weak in their inherent ability to put a man down, so we try to enhance the effect by shooting twice, and 2) in a highly charged situation, the first shot may miss . . . if only by inches. Instantly triggering the second shot takes this possibility into consideration.

Neither of these two possibilities is common with a shotgun; therefore, firing two subsequent shots is not as critical. Also, hitting twice with the shotgun may be slightly more difficult because of its greater recoil and muzzle flip, so if the first shot has not settled the adversary's hash, place the second one right in the command-and-control center! There are few things more disconcerting than to hit an adversary well and solidly with the deadliest CQB weapon extant and find that he is not at all impressed. A subsequent cranial shot will change his mind (pun intended). Another reason to consider the head shot is that the nervous system tends to shut off and disregard any subsequent injury or pain after the first hits, so further shots to the body will probably not help. A cranial hit will disrupt the brain and usually result in a no-reflex kill. Forget that nonsense about shooting the adversary's legs in order to prevent him from shooting you. Plan A: center of mass. Plan B: head shot.

The second method of incapacitation by a shotgun—injury to the central nervous system (i.e., brain)—is quite conclusive. Or as it is commonly phrased: "Place a single round in the data base and turn off the machine!" The cranial application of the shotgun not only "turns off the data base," it demolishes it completely. Although the central nervous system includes the spine, this is generally a less ideal target than the head itself because of the spine's relative size and location within the body (unless the adversary is turned around).

Don't shoot your target and then stand there gawking if he doesn't go down. Even if the head shot solution is not immediately effective, don't despair—shoot him again. Consider also that you might be forced to take shots on individuals turned sideways or partially obscured by light. Additionally, if you have received intelligence that the adversary is either under the influence of a drug or wearing ballistic armor, forget Plan A and go for the head shot immediately.

Selecting the shotgun minimizes the concern over effective stopping power, but you must still remain ready for Plan B if the initial shots have been ineffective. Remember: *there are no guarantees in a gunfight*!

CHAPTER FIVE

SHOTGUN TYPES AND USEFUL ACCESSORIES

"To rely on rustics and not to prepare is the greatest of crimes. To be prepared beforehand for any contingency is the greatest of virtues."

—Ho Yen-Hsi,
Chinese scholar commenting
on Sun Tzu's *Art of War*

The antipersonnel shotgun is available in two types of actions: slide action (aka pump action) and semiautomatic. There are other hybrids available such as the Benelli M3 or SPAS-12, which are achieved by the flip of a switch. There are also bullpup shotguns that put the cart before the horse, so to speak. They are designed to be considerably shorter than standard shotguns by placing the trigger group ahead of the shotgun action. Examples of this include the old High Standard M10 and the Mossberg 500 Bullpup. They accomplish the storage and close-quarters

There are a variety of shotguns available for defensive use, ranging from basic to technologically advanced.

The Benelli Super 90 M3 state-of-the-art defensive shotgun adopted by many tactical teams worldwide.

deployment missions without the hassle of folding stocks or federal entanglements. Finally, even in this age of technology, we still see the basic and ancient double-barrel shotgun. Let's take a close look at each one.

DOUBLE-BARREL

The double-barrel shotgun has much going for it. It is shorter in length than most of its competitors, its manual of arms is so uncomplicated that even the most tactically illiterate can handle it, and, finally, it is faster for the first two shots than anything else on the market. However, the double does have some disadvantages. If you are faced with more than two gorillas, or if you miss with either of the two shots, you are in trouble.

Additionally, unless your double-barrel shotgun has two external hammers (like the old coach guns), there is no truly safe way to keep it loaded in storage. Most double-barrels are designed to cock the hammer on opening—thus instantly compressing the springs—and also to automatically activate the safety when closing. It is either loaded, cocked and ready to go, or its action must be kept empty with the tension relaxed on the internal springs to ensure reliability. With the exposed-hammer double, you can lower the two hammers on the live

33

primers and experience a good balance of safety versus tactical readiness. The double-barrel, so loaded, can be ready to go by simply cocking the hammers without fumbling with a miniscule or poorly placed safety button.

Another asset of the double is instant ammunition selection through trigger selection. It is a simple matter to load one barrel with buckshot (for multipurpose uses) and the other barrel with either birdshot or slug. Many used doubles (either side-by-side or over-under) can be had for a song from the used rack at most gun stores. These will invariably be sporting guns that bear close examination for strength by a gunsmith. Other than lopping off the barrel to comply with the legal 18-inch length (we mustn't cross the feds), no other work needs to be done. The exposed-hammer guns are desirable if you can find them, but others will do as well if you keep their assets and liabilities in mind.

SLIDE-ACTION

The slide-action (or pump-action) shotgun has been in service since the last century. It has many advantages, not the least of which is mechanical reliability. Further, it can operate with ammunition that would choke the most high-tech semiauto shotguns around; it will also do this in varying climatic conditions, or even when proper maintenance has been ignored; it has a capacity of between four and eight rounds and offers a degree of ammunition selection with the appropriate operator technique. It is also one of the more inexpensive weapons that can be added to an arsenal.

The disadvantages of a slide-action are few. The physical act of immediately actuating the "pump" is what allows the operator to fire subsequent shots; therefore, that pumping act must become reflexive upon firing. The most prevalent malfunction observed with a slide-action is the operator-induced "short-stroke"—i.e.,

34

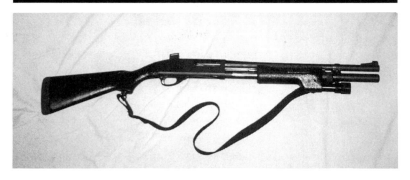

The quintessential tactical shotgun: Smith & Wesson 3000 pump.

not actuating the pump far enough to reload a live round after the expended shell case has been ejected, which results in a *click* instead of *bang!* Very bad show . . . dangerous too, particularly if you were really depending on that bang. The best solution is to turn the full pumping action of the fore-end into a reflex action.

For its intended purpose and in its tactical niche, the slide-action shotgun is hard to beat. Good choices are the ubiquitous Remington 870, the out-of-production Smith & Wesson 3000, and the Mossbergs in military trim.

SEMIAUTOMATIC

The next type of combat shotgun is the semiautomatic. These weapons allow a very slight speed advantage over the slide-actions when the hostile targets are lined up in a row ready for inspection. The speed edge is not so obvious in tactical situations where the location of live adversaries will vary constantly. Another advantage is that the semiauto may be shot repeatedly with one hand, whereas the slide-action must be manually operated with both hands. This situation does not arise often, but in the event of an interior search that demands a free hand to open doors and so forth, the semiauto might be preferable.

35

The Remington 11-87, America's premier semiautomatic shotgun.

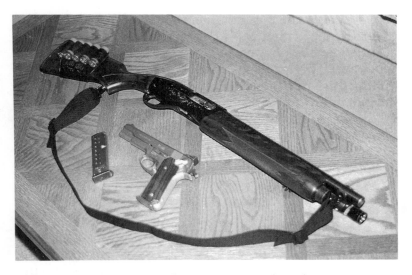

The author carried this sawed-off Remington 1100 during his assignment in a surveillance unit. This weapon had been involved in several gunfights before it was issued to him.

Operator-induced malfunctions are not much of an issue with a semiauto. On the downside is the fact that semiautos won't function with as many types of ammunition as the slide-action, nor will they function as reliably without proper maintenance. Two good semiauto choices are the Benelli tactical shotguns and the Remington 11-87. Beretta also makes a good tactical shotgun.

HYBRID

There are some hybrid shotguns that exhibit both semiautomatic and slide-action capability. This type of setup is ideal for tactical teams that make use of specialty gas and breaching rounds that may not function in an autoloader. An operator can fire the round in question, flip the switch, pump the action to manually reload an antipersonnel round, and then proceed with the mission in semiauto. The only such shotgun worthy of consideration at this writing is the Benelli M3.

PARTS, ACCESSORIES, AND MODIFICATIONS

The shotgun is a tool designed for a mission. Any addition that enhances that mission is worthwhile. If the realistic tactical need for such an addition or modification cannot be explained, then it is probably a bad idea and best avoided. Be particularly careful with accessories designed for competition. Competitive shooters often produce very useful and combat worthy items, but just as often they bring forth gear that is only useful on the shooting range. We need the inventive environment of competition, but we also need to look at any particular product through the eyes of a warrior.

Buttpads

Starting at the bottom, all shotguns need a buttpad. This is not so much to guard against recoil, although it does this well, but rather to keep the shotgun from slipping off the shoulder during firing. The shotgun's position on the shoulder, as with the hand-grip index on a holstered pistol, has a great effect on the results of your shooting (that means hits). The buttpad ensures that the index, once obtained, will not be lost by accident because of slippage. Whatever pad you choose, it is important to have it rounded off at the heel and around its outer edges to avoid catching on your clothing during the mounting procedure. The Pachmayr Decelerator is a preferred brand.

Extra Ammo Carriers

Sometimes an operator will find that having an extra ammunition source on the shotgun is desirable in the event of a 0'dark-thirty grab-and-go scenario. There are situations where a few extra rounds will be worth their weight in diamonds. The two most prevalent methods of keeping extra ammunition on the weapon are the stock-mounted cuff and the receiver-mounted sidesaddle. Each has certain advantages over the other, and both tend to slightly unbalance the shotgun. You really must weigh the need against liability factors with this one.

A Sparks Cold Comfort cheekpiece is used to carry extra ammunition on the shotgun stock.

MD Labs' two-shell belt pouches as seen alone and on a tactical belt.

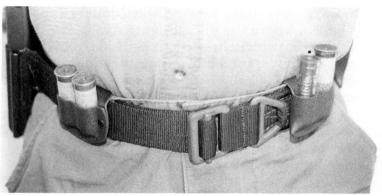

A better option might be to use one (or two) Kydex shell pouches. These small, lightweight, thermoplastic rigid shell pouches use the inherent spring rate of the Kydex material to hold the rounds in place, yet allow instantaneous retrieval. The pouches are impervious to water, salt, solvents, sweat . . . and, yes, even blood.

Stocks

There are almost as many different types of stock configurations as there are criminals in Los Angeles. The most useful and versatile is the standard stock that comes from the factory. The primary consideration is the length of the stock. An operator with long arms can make do with a short stock but not the other way around (not very efficiently anyway). If you are dealing with an agency weapon that is issued to you, there is no option but to adapt to it. But if the shotgun is a personal weapon, the length of the stock can be easily modified to fit. What you must look for is the ability to shoulder the stock easily without having to overextend your arms. An old shotgunner's fit check is to place the butt into the inside bend of the elbow and then check for proper finger placement on the trigger. If the stock is too long for your arms, you will have difficulty reaching the trigger. I would say that perhaps half of the tactical shotgunners I've seen could benefit from a slightly shorter stock.

If a shotgunner will be part of a tactical unit, a pistol-grip-stock configuration has certain advantages. This is obvious when one hand will be needed to manage mission-essential gear or to open doors while retaining the ability to manage the shotgun and shoot (one-handed). There are also many folding-stock options available. Folding stocks are only useful if the shotgun is to be carried and deployed from a small vehicle, carried in a

Smith & Wesson 3000 with a folding stock.

With the stock folded, this makes for a very compact weapon.

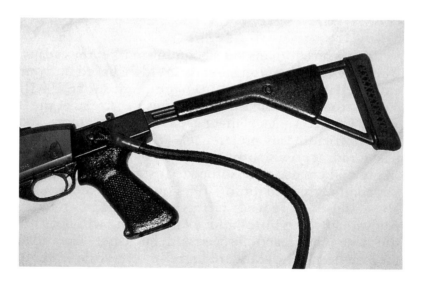

The folding stock itself must be solid in the folded or open positions.

covert format, or used in extremely close quarters. The folder is not nearly as easy or comfortable to use as a standard stock. If a folder is chosen, select one that has positive "open" and "closed" positions and that has the least amount of motion when it is open. Check it for sharp edges. I remember when my partner and I were issued a short-barreled 870 with a Remington factory "over the top" folding stock. My partner loaded up and began a multiple-target drill. When he was done, he commented that the stock was not very comfortable. His comments were punctuated by droplets of blood spattering on the floor of the range . . . from the cut on his right cheek!

Enlarged Safety Button

Enlarged safety buttons are useful. Keep in mind that if you will be called to use a shotgun that is not so equipped, the standard safety button may be more difficult to disengage if you've become accustomed to the larger variety.

Sights

Sights on shotguns are a booming market these days. The type of sights you select should be based on your expected use of the shotgun. A simple front bead will suffice from handshake distances out to the end of the B Zone. These come in plain brass, a rainbow of colors, and even in tritium (my preference). Tritium is a hydrogen-based radioactive isotope that gives off a slight glow. Many makers use this isotope to install their aftermarket sights intended for low-light operations. If *any* slug shooting is expected, rifle sights are the answer. Additionally, the installation of rifle sights will not hurt the close-range reaction speed with buckshot. They are a no-lose item. The standard barrel-mounted rifle sights will do, but the Jeff Cooper-rediscovered ghost ring sights are the best choice by far. This system is even available with a tritium-equipped front sight for those nocturnal activities requiring them. The ghost ring sight is a thin-rimmed aperture sight. When it is peered through to align the front sight, it tends to disappear from the visual focus. When used with a standard rifle-type front sight, the ghost ring allows you to keep both eyes open when shooting. It matches the speed of a bead-equipped gun up close and allows greater accuracy in delivering the slug.

Fore-Ends

There are a myriad of fore-ends available for the shotgun. The polymer variety (as with the buttstock) are much more robust than wooden ones and are a good addition. There are dedicated flashlight housing/fore-ends available for a variety of shotguns. This is one of the most useful inventions I've ever seen. Target identification is essential when operating in a reduced-light environment, and these tactical light fore-ends provide this capability.

Magazine Extensions

Magazine extensions are available to extend the shotgun's capacity from four to eight or more. These are simple screw-on affairs that extend from the existing tube out to the muzzle, thereby making room for extra rounds. These kits provide a spring that is longer and stronger than the factory original. One advantage of the extended magazine is to enable the operator to load one or two rounds down from full capacity in order to provide room for the introduction of a different ammunition type (such as a slug).

Slings

Slings are another item worth considering. Slings are mandatory during most shotgun training courses for a safety margin during class discussions. When the instructor orders "sling up," he can be reasonably certain that everyone's muzzle is not covering anything it should not. Slings are also useful at times when the hands will be otherwise occupied momentarily. There is just no practical way to retain the shotgun and yet keep your hands free other than a sling. The slings available today vary from simple nylon or leather carrying straps to the multipurpose tactical slings.

One interesting sling system is the Tactical Quick Sling. This sling is actually a 35- to 48-inch length of 3/8-inch woven bungee cord that can be attached to any weapon by its two black, spring-steel split rings. The ends are secured with 3M shrink-wrap, creating a no-catch effect so that the bungee sling does not catch on tactical vests, architectural features, or uniform items (such as badges or nameplates). Also, the sling stretches to 250 percent of its original length, allowing a variety of shooting positions and yet maintaining continuous weapon retention. These bungee slings were originally designed for quickly deploying and securing breaching shotguns, but they are equally useful for any close-quarters long-gun application.

Chokes

Choke systems are one of the most requested gun-smith modifications for shotguns. A choke acts to con-

The polychoke device described in the text.

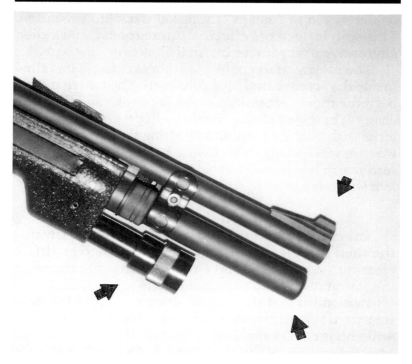

The business end of a tactical shotgun. Notice the front sight, magazine extension, and tactical flashlight.

strict the shotgun bore and thereby tighten or open the shot pattern. The operating principle is the same as a pressure nozzle constricting the water flow through a garden hose. Too much choke will cause flyers with buckshot and erratic performance with slugs. Gunsmiths who specialize in the tactical shotgun have ironed the bugs out of the choking systems and can give you just what is needed.

Some shooters use screw-in chokes to calibrate what they need. This is fine if only one ammunition type will be used, but if any slugs are to be fired, the screw-in choke will eventually accompany the slug downrange. Another alternative is the polychoke device that actually allows you to "dial in" the amount of choke required. This simple device is effective, quite robust, and a good alternative to expensive internal chokes or new barrels.

The most popular choke systems are those installed inside the actual barrel by a gunsmith. The two that have been the most successful are the jug choke and the Vang choke. These two choke systems will provide tighter patterns with buckshot without affecting the accuracy of the weapon when using slugs. If your new shotgun won't pattern worth beans, an internal choke may solve the problem without having to scrap the barrel.

Miscellaneous

Other modifications that may be useful are slotting the shell lifter (particularly on older guns) to facilitate clearing a double feed and an action job if the trigger or the action itself is unmanageable as is.

Remember that the tactical shotgun is a tool intended for a particular mission. If an accessory or modification will enhance its capability to handle the mission, then buy it regardless of the cost. But if it does nothing for the weapon's ability to handle its mission, it is only a worthless piece of junk.

CHAPTER SIX

DEVELOPING THE "COMBAT" FRAME OF MIND

"Every man that knows the power of joy in battle, knows what it is like when the wolf rises in the heart."

—Theodore Roosevelt,
The Works of Theodore Roosevelt, Vol. XII

Of far more importance than armament or marksmanship skill is the cultivation of the warrior's attitude. A cornerstone of this attitude is the realization that there are seemingly harmless people in the world who would kill you (and probably your family as well) with as much thought as they would devote to lighting a cigarette. Such things are quite common today, and this knowledge should breed a certain alertness and a general suspicion of strangers.

Because you cannot go around pointing your shotguns at every suspicious-

"The Guru," Colonel Jeff Cooper, as he addresses a group of his students during a defensive shotgun course at Old Gunsite.

looking character you encounter, a system of escalating readiness and responsiveness must be adopted. Such a system must also provide a method for overcoming the natural reluctance to harm another human being. Few people would argue against killing a man who is obviously trying to kill you, but there is often a clear and sometimes fatal hesitation by many to "drop the hammer" at the moment of truth.

Therefore, a truly practical system of combat mindcraft would provide a way to both enhance your alertness and provide a method to morally surmount the societal and emotional barriers to justifiable homicide. Such a

Mind-set and attitude are more important than marksmanship.

system is already available. It is Colonel Jeff Cooper's Combat Mind-Set and Color Code of Readiness System.

Of all the teachers of martial thought, none is more renowned than Jeff Cooper. His system is the greatest development in the field of personal combat since the

49

invention of the sword. Cooper devised and implemented a Color Code of Readiness system that describes a four-level progression of increasing readiness. This system is easy to understand and equally easy to implement in daily life.

Along with enhanced awareness, the combat mind-set makes it possible to overcome the natural disinclination to harm another man by enhancing your ability to recognize an attack and your readiness to respond. Many people, when faced with a deadly enemy, lapse into disbelief. When they are looking death in the face, they might say something like, "That hoodlum isn't really raising that awful knife and coming at me . . . is he?" These gentle folks, and there are many of them, seem inclined to try and bargain their way out of a battle to the death. The combat mind-set helps us to rise above such an emotional-mental block and take care of the business at hand . . . specifically, *front sight—press!* When facing death, a properly organized person might instead think, "Aha, that suspicious-looking character over there has a knife in his hand, and he is coming toward me in an aggressive manner . . . I'm ready for him. Boy, won't he be surprised!" Adopting the combat mind-set helps develop such an attitude.

The underlying theme is alertness. A fighting man must always be attentive to his surroundings, actually looking for possible enemies, lest he be taken by surprise. Such alertness is not paranoia by any means, just an acceptance of the fact that we live in a violent world.

Ignoring your surroundings, or as Cooper says, "being in Condition White," is asking to get blindsided by an attacker. We all lapse into the inattentive limbo of Condition White daily, but we can only afford to do so when asleep behind the locked gates of our homes. Never let your mind drift away when you are out in public. If you do, no level of skill or amount of ammunition will save you if you are attacked!

50

With such a commitment, keeping a pistol strapped to your side is not unreasonable. In higher-risk environments (or where pistols are unavailable) keeping a fighting shotgun handy is even more reasonable because we realize that trouble may come at any time. This mental state is called Condition Yellow and is characterized by "relaxed alertness."

In Condition Yellow you have generally anticipated that a fight *might* occur, but not when or against whom. You are aware of your surroundings and take particular notice of anything out of the ordinary. You notice the occupants of vehicles next to you at stoplights. You take note of any persons whose actions might seem to be keyed to yours and visually identify what they have in their hands. In Condition Yellow you cannot be surprised, because you are alert for possible trouble and your conditioned response is there (like your weapon), just in case.

The appearance of a *possible* threat propels you to the next level of readiness, which is identified as Condition Orange. In Condition Orange you do not know for certain that a fight is imminent, but you have your suspicions—and the presence of a possible enemy, *right there*, is reason enough.

The transition from Yellow to Orange is paramount to decreasing reaction time and allowing you to perceive the threat when it develops. An example of such a transition would be if the occupants of the vehicle next to yours in the traffic jam began to aggressively exhibit gang signs to you with their hands or if the individual you noticed with the weapon outlined under his clothing began to follow you. The main difference between the general alertness of Yellow and the specific alertness of Orange is that you are now focused on, and expecting trouble from, one particular source. You are actively looking for the clues that might confirm the ill intent of your potential enemy.

51

The instant that you realize and actually accept that a fight is now quite likely, you've entered Condition Red. For example, if the gang members in the adjoining vehicle begin to get out of their car and approach you, or if the individual following you with the weapon outlined under his clothes reaches under his shirt for it, you are in Red. In Condition Red you've already decided that the situation may require a lethal response, although you may not necessarily need to employ it. You've made up your mind to shoot if the enemy commits any life-threatening action, and all systems are *go!*

The ability to perceive such a specific and deadly threat, recognize it as such, and react to it is facilitated by the conscious establishment of a "mental trigger." This mental trigger is a preestablished mental reaction to fight, which is activated by the initiation of any lethal aggression on the part of the adversary. This process is reactive in nature and requires extreme attention to the enemy's actions. Having planned responses to threats will prevent the confusion that many people experience when they must *think* out their responses before acting them out. A planned response is a decision that has already been made, so there will not be any hesitation before the fact.

Examples of the mental trigger would be as follows: the hypothetical gang members that exited their car begin to approach you and are brandishing several weapons, and you are unable to drive away because of heavy traffic. Or the armed man following you produces a pistol and begins to raise it . . . *toward you!* The only prudent solution is to stop the action with your own gunfire. If your rules of engagement require a verbal warning of any sort, this is the time to issue it. The only further step is *front sight—press!*

When you realize that deadly threat, it must trigger your own terminal response. The *only* programmed response to a threat on your life must be to shoot. With enough training, this becomes an issue of action and reaction where your killing stroke is irrevocably triggered by the lethal aggressive actions of the criminal. Too bad for him! Only certain preset safety checks will prevent your shots. For example, if the man with a gun also has a badge visible, or if the aggressive gang members throw down their weapons and run away when you offer resistance, you do not fire.

I remember one instance where the preset safety check saved the day. A gang member armed with a machete was running toward me (Condition Red). He kept coming after being ordered to stop, and I consciously made the decision to shoot him (mental trigger). I remember shifting my visual focus to the front sight. I was about to press the trigger and drop him, when my well-meaning partner accidentally stepped between my muzzle and the suspect. My front sight was no longer superimposed on the bad guy, but on the navy blue field that was my partner's back! I held my fire (preset safety check). By the grace of God, my partner came through unscathed, and we solved the problem at hand. Training won the day, but we were also quite lucky . . . especially my partner.

With practice and correct mental programming, you can respond to a lethal threat with a conditioned reflex. Limiting your response options to a lethal threat will cut down reaction time dramatically. I believe that you can control your specific behavior by deciding that you will react as you've trained yourself to react. If you are concentrating on solving the immediate problem, you will not have time to think about the actual danger you are in, and you will probably minimize many of the physical manifestations of stress.

But that is not the end of the tale. The subject of supposed "after-action remorse," or post-operational trauma (POT as Jeff Cooper calls it), has been extensively refuted in earlier writings. That particular horse is dead, and further flogging will only damage the meat. Suffice it to say that if you are the least bit squeamish about blasting a low-life predatory criminal, nothing herein will help you. If, on the other hand, you refuse to be a victim at any level and have accepted responsibility for your own safety, then you've already got your mind on the right track. That alone, mixed with liberal doses of alertness, tactical training, and the combat mind-set, will allow you to maintain control of your environment and of yourself before, during, and after the fight. Programming after-action attitudes, just as we program prefight and in-fight attitudes, will also make you view your subsequent victory in its appropriate light.

Having achieved this mental outlook, when the last shot has been fired, and the last goblin falls onto the clammy tarmac, you will likely feel pleased and proud at having survived—no, not just survived—rather, at having *won!* Make no mistake: this is no time to feel remorse over having killed another. To be remorseful requires having done wrong. Successfully defending your country, your loved ones, or yourself (in order of importance) is cause for pride, not sorrow. As my friend Jeff Cooper said, "There is nothing wrong with winning, and there is a great deal wrong with losing."

Before the fight we must be alert, ready, and willing to fight—if we must. During the fight we concentrate fully and exclusively on solving the tactical problem at hand. After the fight we will feel proud at having won, pleased to be alive, and glad that we were suitably armed. That's all there is to it! If this annoys any bleeding-heart, touchie-feelie, feel-good, felon-huggers out there, then too bad because their ramblings will not change reality!

CHAPTER SEVEN

PROGRAMMING PHYSICAL AND MENTAL RESPONSES

"In war the only sure defense is offense, and the efficiency of offense depends upon the warlike souls of those conducting it."

—General George S. Patton, Requoted from *Cooper's Commentaries* by Jeff Cooper

The thought processes that a man experiences prior to, during, and immediately after a fight to the death are a fascinating topic that will one day inspire serious scientific study. As one who has experienced some of these thought processes a number of times, I have given their examination great attention.

In times of extreme alarm many people experience a series of physical effects resulting from their apprehension of the situation before them. This apprehension causes the adrenal glands to flush the system with primal adrenaline, resulting in an

55

increased heart rate. This is accompanied by a similarly increasing level of performance, to a certain point. After that point, performance deteriorates rapidly.

This performance curve is called the inverted-U hypothesis. This theory was first proposed in 1908 by Yerkes and Dodson in an attempt to explain the relationship between arousal and performance. Their theory describes a bell-like curve that symbolizes the increased levels of stress and performance climbing together to a certain point. Beyond this point, any further increase in stress will lead to diminished performance, they reasoned. Their predicted relationship between stress and performance was curvilinear, taking the shape of an inverted U.

There are many other individual studies that attempt to explain how and why arousal (or stress) affects performance levels. They all seem to arrive at the same conclusion: that stress is essential to high levels of performance, but too much stress is detrimental to it. The heart rate seems to have a great influence on these performance levels. As we all know, life-threatening alarm tends to increase the heart rate. Optimum performance seems to occur when the heart rate is between 115 and 145 beats per minute (BPM). When 145 BPM is exceeded, fine motor control begins to diminish in the hands. The reason for this is biological. When a man begins to experience extreme alarm, the body forces the blood from the extremities and allows it to collect in the large muscles. Originally, this may have served to allow greater strength when facing saber-toothed tigers and cave bears, as well as to attempt to prevent death from blood loss if one of these critters bit off a caveman's hand.

When you reach 175 BPM, and your heart rate sounds like a passable imitation of a Browning .50-caliber machine gun, all you have left are simple push-and-pull skills. At this point, you may also experience perceptual narrowing. This physical effect causes substantial

You will react in combat as you've programmed yourself to react.

decrease in peripheral vision as the senses focus in on the actual threat and disregard what is around it.

Extreme stress will also affect the ability to make quick critical decisions—such as which reloading technique to use or what shooting position to adopt. An early theorist on the subject, Dr. Hick, proposed that response options should be kept to a minimum (Hick's Law). He found that every additional response option actually increased reaction time by as much as 50 percent. The reason, he explained, is that every additional response option must be "examined" by the mind and either selected or discarded prior to final execution. Even though this difference in response time will be minute, the delay might just be substantial enough to die from.

For these reasons, fighting techniques must emphasize simple, direct movements that are effective in spite of the possible physical states you might encounter during times of trouble. Additionally, these techniques must take such physical effects into consideration as well as be made reflexive through extensive practice and repetition.

57

Many of these physical effects may, however, be attenuated by a proper mental attitude as well as with constant tactical training. The goal is not to prevent reactions to stress, but rather to keep them under control. Developing a strong cardiovascular system, for example, will allow your body to operate comfortably at higher levels of stress. In addition, a fit body will be able to recover from these effects much faster than an unfit body.

Much of the mental anxiety associated with physical combat may be alleviated by conducting continual and proper physical, as well as tactical, training. This constant practice will develop self-confidence, which in turn will promote calmness under fire. About 200 A.D., the Chinese feudal general Wang Ling wrote, "If officers are unaccustomed to rigorous drilling they will be worried and hesitant in battle; if generals are not thoroughly trained they will inwardly quail when they face the enemy." As we are nearing the 21st century, nothing has changed in this regard.

The physical effects of a calm mental state are a stable heart rate and a feeling of control, both of which are much needed in a fight. This is exactly the opposite effect from that experienced from the uncontrolled feelings of fear and panic. Facing a capable enemy with a calm and controlled attitude, and winning because of it, is one of the great experiences of man.

The tempo of events in a fight will often preclude any response that must be preceded by a conscious thought. This requires a reflexive response to a threat. This immediate counterattack comes from "hard-wiring" the physical skills you are training into the nervous system. Bill Burroughs of Sigarms coined the term *hard-wire* to describe the continual, repetitive training involved in programming a physical skill into your neurological system, thereby making it a reflexive skill. The nervous system connections required to execute a particular movement can be enhanced by extensive repetition. Along with this hard-wiring, or "reflexizing" of a physical skill, the analytical mind must also be educated about why the skill is necessary and how it fits into the tactical big picture. An example could be explaining why an emergency reload is executed the way it is, explaining how it fits a certain tactical need (soft-wiring), and then practicing it 5,000 times in succession (hard-wiring) to develop the needed muscle memory for its reflexive execution.

When first programming a reflexive motor skill, you must practice it in a step-by-step staccato fashion to ensure that every essential element is included (such as disengaging safeties and keeping fingers off triggers). These static repetitions develop the initial neural connections.

After the static performance becomes comfortable, you may begin to "round off the edges" and make the entire execution more fluid. Do not attempt to speed things up . . . not yet. Speed is not an issue at this juncture, only developing smoothness of action. The length of these two phases may vary depending on individual skill, but moving on to the next phase without having established a comfort level in the previous phase would be a waste of time.

The third phase is dynamic training. At this point, the action is executed at a reasonable speed. The level of speed is dependent on the skill of the shooter and on the difficulty of the problem (balancing speed and accuracy, remember that one?).

At this third phase, begin to introduce a threat stimulus, such as the sudden appearance of a hostile target or multiple hostile targets, in order to associate the motor skill with a reaction to a threat. Eventually, the subconscious mind will think of it in terms of an inseparable action-reaction (or stimulus-response), and this will decrease reaction time.

Additionally, training situations that require responses to threat stimuli automatically begin to raise the

All the targets should represent the human adversaries you will likely face. Here we see simple "pepper poppers" painted to resemble humans. This is not the perfect solution, but it is on the right track.

arousal level. Training in such an emotionally charged environment will begin to desensitize you to the state of extreme alarm inevitable in personal combat, and it will also begin to develop self-confidence. Confidence is crucial to shooting success in combat situations.

Developing a combat mind-set allows the conscious mind to prepare before the fact—for the probability of personal combat. Programming the proper physical responses to a threat enables us to react quickly and decisively with ferocity of spirit and violence of action during the fight. But this is only part of the package.

Many people are bombarded from all points on the compass with the misinformation that they'll feel terrible remorse if they drop their assailant and win the fight. The human mind is very receptive to all types of input, and if you hear something enough times (even lies), you will actually start to believe it. You will become "programmed" or brainwashed to believe it. This foolishness has produced an entire generation of armed pseudowarriors ready to fall down in tears the first time they must shoot for blood.

60

With a little work, this can be changed. Professional athletes have been using the tool of mental imagery for years to enhance their physical performance and control negative thoughts.

Mental imagery, or visualization, has been proven to enhance the neural connections used during actual physical performance. We can use this same meditative daydream to visualize the before and during phases of a physical fight exactly as we would like to handle it. This same method can be extremely useful for developing proper after-action attitudes. Just as you hard-wire the actual physical reflexes into your neural pathways, you can program thought patterns into your mind based on how you would like to perceive reality. The better and more vivid you are able to imagine an event, the stronger the effect on the subconscious mind. Each person's perception of the world is, in his own mind, a reality. The actual reality is immutable, but the way you view it can change. For example, you can be fairly certain that World War I hero Sergeant Alvin York viewed the world much differently than a 1960s pot-smoking "flower child" did. How we view the world dictates how we react to it. Such combat mindcraft can enhance your physical skills and reactions, stop negative thinking during combat, ensure better performance, and prevent guilty feelings after the fight is over, regardless of what you are told by others.

There is nothing mystical about this "tactical daydream." It is the same sort of daydream that children entertain themselves with during a boring class in school. Simply play out a situation in your head from beginning to end and mentally handle it in the way you would like to do so in real life. For example, your daydream might go something like this: you see the bad guy approaching with an upraised knife in his hand, bloody from his last victim. Your programmed response to this perceived threat is to bring your shotgun up, disengage the safety, and challenge the advancing hostile. He

61

ignores you and keeps coming, increasing his speed and raising the knife for the intended slash. He screams some foul and unintelligible curse as you sidestep quickly and visually pick up the front sight. There is no need for negotiations or discussions. He started it, and you *know* exactly what he intends to do. The bottom line—your life—is more important than his. You press the trigger twice and, keeping the muzzle in place, look over the top of the shotgun to check on his status. He is down. You've smacked him dead center with two charges of buckshot. His knife has clattered harmlessly on what is now a puddle of his own blood. It's over. You are alive, and he is not. You make the necessary notifications (police, personal attorney, etc.) and maintain a low profile for the kinder-gentler folks in the crowd. Inside, however, you notice that you feel pleased and proud at having remained in control, at having reacted as you'd trained, and at having ended the career of a violent attacker who might have chosen a less prepared person the next time—end of story! Do you think that this same scenario could be viewed differently by a noncombatant personality? Of course it could. Do noncombatant personalities fare well in personal combat? No, they simply die.

You are a product of your thoughts and your perceptions of the world. During times of intense conflict, your analytical processes may not be able to keep up with the tempo of events. Programming canned physical reactions and thought processes—triggered by your perceptions of danger—will help your combat efficiency immensely. Additionally, programming proper after-action thinking will negate any trace of the postoperational trauma syndrome. Such complete training will help you to know when those physical skills are needed and to implement them reflexively. It will also help you view their successful deployment in a more realistic light.

CHAPTER EIGHT

READY (TO SHOOT) POSITIONS

"I never allowed a man to get the drop on me."
—"Wild Bill" Hickok,
The Black Hills

Shotgun-carry methods and ready positions should mirror your level of readiness for a fight. Because the shotgun is not worn on a belt, as is a pistol, it generally takes a conscious understanding that combat is likely before you think to retrieve it. If the level of readiness and the expectation of violence are high, you would carry the shotgun in hand in a manner that facilitates an instant reaction. Sometimes, however, even though the shotgun is in hand, trouble is not immediately expected, and you can relax the level of readiness slightly.

Other times, you may be merely transporting the weapon from one location to another with no expectation of attack, and you can use sling carry. The lowest degree of readiness is the administrative carry typified by the "cruiser ready" shotgun secured in a gunrack or closet. Although you may not have the weapon in hand, you know its location and the most expeditious way of getting it into action if you are threatened.

SLING CARRY

Sling carry is similar in practice to holstered carry for a pistol. The weapon is there if necessary, but not without some effort. There are three basic sling carry positions: the American carry, African carry, and tactical carry.

American Carry

In the American carry, the shotgun is carried muzzle up with the sling over the dominant-side shoulder and the dominant hand gripping the sling. To dismount the shotgun from this position, push the dominant hand (and sling) forward while simultaneously reaching under the dominant arm and grabbing the fore-end with the support hand. Then simply push the muzzle toward the target with the support hand and remove the dominant arm from between the

The American carry sling position.

64

front sling swivel and the support arm. As the support arm clears, regrasp the pistol grip and then simply complete the mounting process. The whole operation takes about two seconds—quite a long time if the goblins are charging your position with fixed bayonets—but it is far preferable to doing nothing.

One distinct disadvantage of the American carry is quickly noticed by those favoring dominant-side hip carry of sidearms. The comb and heel of the shotgun stock is constantly striking, scratching, and otherwise scraping against the pistol's rear sight. This is most deleterious to the pistol sight or shotgun stock (especially if this unlikely marriage drifts the rear sight's setting as it did on one of my colleague's pistols). Alternatives? Switch to a crossdraw carry for your pistol or the African carry for the shotgun.

The African carry sling position.

African Carry

The African carry involves carrying the shotgun muzzle down, slung over the support-side shoulder. This mode of carry, I am told, is quite popular in—you guessed it—Africa. An added bonus with this mode of carry is that it seems to be less visible than the American carry (we mustn't upset the kinder-gentler folks, you know). Additionally, the African carry is somewhat faster to the shoulder since the support hand already rests naturally on its normal spot on the fore-end to steady the slung weapon. All that is needed to dismount and orient the weapon is a simple forward movement of the arm coupled with an outboard motion of the wrist. This motion is simultaneous with the dominant hand reaching across the abdomen to secure the pistol grip and finally pulling the stock into the shoulder. The elapsed time is less than two seconds.

Tactical Carry

A third sling carry method that has become popular with the door-kicking crowd is the tactical carry. The tactical carry is undoubtedly the fastest sling carry method from which to deploy the shotgun, and it is suitable for any level of readiness. In this method the shotgun hangs across the chest or to the side in a muzzle-down position from a specially designed sling. This position is most useful when one or both hands will be needed to deploy explosive breaching devices, open doors, assist teammates, etc. It is also useful for weapon-retention purposes during violent physical activity. Primarily, this method differs from the others in that the shotgun does not need to be unslung before it can be fired. Rather it can be mounted and fired while the sling is still in position.

The tactical sling carry.

IN-HAND CARRY

Low-Profile Carry

There will be times when you have a nonsling-equipped shotgun in hand

The low-profile (pocket) carry.

Cradle carry.

with no expectation of imminent combat. One useful carry method for such applications is low-profile carry, where the shotgun is cradled in the dominant hand around the rear of the receiver with the index finger along the pistol grip and the thumb around the rear of the trigger guard. If the situation becomes prolonged, you may hook the thumb of the dominant hand into the pants pocket or gunbelt to ease the burden on the arm. Mounting the shotgun from this carry position involves securing the fore-end with the support hand and subsequently mounting the shotgun up to the shoulder in the usual manner.

Moderate-Risk Carry

The next level of carry/ readiness involves circumstances where there is a much greater perception of danger, such that any form of low-risk carry is not indicated. You must have the shotgun in hand, expecting the possibility of hostile contact, but you

67

won't have any indications that it might occur any time soon. Carry methods here must be a compromise between readiness and long-term convenience and can be labeled moderate-risk carry.

Rhodesian Ready

The primary moderate-risk carry method is called Rhodesian ready. It involves putting both hands on the shotgun in their firing positions. The dominant hand is held more or less at the belt level with the buttstock along the forearm. The support hand grips the fore-end, and the arm is relaxed, depressing the muzzle toward the deck at about the 11:00 position. This is a low-energy ready position that is not physically taxing. It falls between the low profile of sling carry and the ready-to-engage positions. In such environments, the shotgun is carried with the safety on. Dealing with the safety must become an ingrained part of the mount-and-fire routine (more on this later).

Taylor Underarm Assault Position

To react to an unexpected threat from the Rhodesian ready, simply move the muzzle toward the perceived threat and mount the shotgun in the standard manner as usual. The response time is about 1.5 seconds, but for reaction shooting at spitball distances, a better and faster option is the Taylor underarm assault position as developed by none other

The Rhodesian ready position for use in casual alert.

68

The Taylor underarm assault position.

than Chuck Taylor. This position involves tucking the buttstock high into the armpit against the pectoral muscle, with the butt itself just inside the armpit. Simultaneously orient the muzzle onto the target with both arms bent and the elbows pointed toward the deck. The physical posture is aggressively forward, but not overtly leaning. It is important to keep the master eye directly over the shotgun barrel so that what the eye sees, the muzzle covers. Since no use of the actual gun's sights takes place, the shotgun is indexed by using the body's position as a solid gun mount. This works admirably for coarse shooting up to 7 meters. Beyond this, conventional shoulder firing and aiming are required.

High-Risk Carry

As you progress up the ladder of readiness and expectation of combat, you will encounter circumstances where you must be an eyeblink away from the shot. Such situations will often have mental, emotional, and physical readiness on Condition Red as you wait and actively look for the threat cue to trigger the killing response. Other times, the perception of threat will keep you in Orange, and subsequently farther away (psychologically speaking) from deadly force. In either case, you want to place the shotgun in a position that allows the greatest degree of visibility, yet minimize the time between

69

recognition of, and reaction to, a threat with a quick snap shot. These are the tactical ready positions.

High-Ready

The first such position is the high-ready (sometimes also called outdoor-ready). This is a modification of the old port arms carry. The high-ready places the muzzle in an elevated position just under the line of sight, in line with the eye and the target. The buttstock is held at approximately belt level or slightly higher and along the dominant-side forearm. The trigger finger is out of the trigger guard and resting on the safety button (depending on the shotgun model, the thumb may be resting on the safety lever), prepared to disengage it. Sometimes, a southpaw will be handed a weapon that is not suitable for left-handed use because of the positioning of the safety button (and other controls). In such cases, you may either eschew the safety button altogether (and religiously observe rule three), or keep the shotgun action slightly open (about 1 inch) and close upon shooting. I prefer the former alternative.

When you recognize the need to shoot, snap the shotgun toward the threat as if thrusting the muzzle into it. Simultaneously, bring the buttstock into the shoulder pocket and disengage the safety. The support elbow should point straight down as much as possible to prevent lateral movement of the muzzle. The dominant

The high-ready position.

70

elbow must be raised sufficiently to create a "pocket" in the shoulder musculature in which the shotgun butt will rest. Avoid exaggerating the position of the dominant elbow. An angle of 30 to 45 degrees will do. The timing for the shot involves pulling the butt into the shoulder a millisecond before firing the shot. The sensation is that the butt has been pulled into the shoulder pocket with the pull of the trigger finger. This is very quick: mount, verify sight alignment, shoot. Time to the shot is about 1.5 seconds.

The high-ready is preferred for negotiating large areas, particularly outdoors where there is no close-quarters/weapon-retention hazard. I've found that it is also quite useful for situations where hostilities are likely from higher ground, such as from second- and third-story windows (i.e., urban apartment buildings). Additionally, the high-ready is generally less fatiguing than other high-risk positions for long-term searches or perimeter posts. Using a high-ready is not wise if hostile contact is expected from lower levels, or if close-quarters hazards exist (such as those found indoors).

Low-Ready

An alternative to the high-ready is the low-ready (also called muzzle-depressed ready). This position already has the shotgun mounted in the shoulder pocket, but the muzzle is lowered from the "on target" position. The degree of muzzle depression depends on the distance to the threat. This is the position to use when you are on the hunt, searching for a hostile. Generally, the muzzle should be in a position where you can still see an adversary's hands and waistband, but not so far that a shot will be substantially delayed. Sometimes the question arises about a safety problem regarding rule two (never point a firearm at anything you are not willing to destroy). Does this mean that you are going to point the shotgun at the lower portion of the adversary's body? Darn right it does!

The low-ready position.

The "hunt" position used when covering a threat.

Are you willing to *destroy* this adversary if he presents a threat? You'd sure better be!

As usual, the trigger finger is off the trigger and positioned to disengage the safety. You will be scanning for a threat, and where the eyes scan, the muzzle scans as well. When the expected threat appears, raise the muzzle as you disengage the safety. When the sights interpose between the eye and the target, look through the rear sight *at the front sight*, and shoot. The low-ready is best for short-duration close-quarters tactical moving and searching, or when hostiles are expected to be at a lower level than the shooter. It works very well indoors with a short shotgun. Its chief drawback is that it's somewhat fatiguing for long-term deployment unless a tactical sling is used or the support arm is rested against the duty belt.

The low-ready and the hunt positions are particularly useful in rapidly moving scenarios.

The indoor low-ready is for use in extreme close quarters such as inside a building.

A variation of this ready position is the indoor-ready (or extreme low-ready). This was developed for circumstances when an extreme close-quarters problem would cause the muzzle to precede the shotgun into unsecured space if a standard low-ready position was used, thereby announcing your arrival. The indoor-ready depresses the muzzle to an extreme degree, where the support hand is actually almost touching the support-side leg, and the muzzle is off to the support side. Regardless of the position used, clearing extremely tight areas with a shotgun is not an easy task.

A viable alternative is to let the shotgun hang from the tactical sling, draw the pistol, and negotiate that particular obstacle with the more manageable pistol. If the shotgun is slingless, you may wish to switch to the

The tactical sling allows the easy transition from shotgun to pistol.

underarm assault position. Place the stock up under the arm as far back as your anatomy will allow. This usually places the dominant hand's thumb joint against the ribs. Moving behind the shotgun muzzle is now considerably easier and safer for the close-quarters environment.

The degree of threat perception is a result of a well-developed combat mind-set and is enhanced by the Color Code of Readiness. And as you can see, this degree of preparedness also dictates how you will carry and handle the shotgun.

CHAPTER NINE

SIGHT PICTURES AND SNAP SHOTS

"In battle the only bullets that count are those that hit."
—Theodore Roosevelt,
The Works of Theodore Roosevelt, Vol. XII

Except for situations where you can literally touch an adversary with the gun muzzle, using shotgun sight(s) is essential if you hope to hit anything. There are those who claim that a shotgun must be pointed instinctively and not aimed. Don't you believe it. Yes, there are times when confrontations will occur so close that you can smell your adversary's bad breath at the end of your muzzle, and, therefore, a rough index of the shotgun (through the shooting position) will suffice without sight verification. But any shots beyond this distance must be sighted.

The consistent placement of the cheek on the stock is paramount to effective snap shooting.

It is important to realize that the sights are not used to align the weapon. The shooting position itself, resulting from a proper shoulder mount, is what actually *aligns* the weapon on target. The sights are used to verify and, if necessary, refine the existence of that alignment for the shot.

As defined in the *The Tactical Pistol*, the flash sight picture is a brief glimpse of the front sight through the rear sight for the purpose of verifying the existing alignment of the weapon in relation to the target. The story does not change when the weapon is a shotgun.

The amount of time that you can take to verify the alignment that your shoulder mount has created is determined by your distance from the adversary. The closer you are to the adversary, the less time you have available to flatten him before he does the same to you. Conversely, the farther away you are from the threat, the more time available to you to hit him. The rule of thumb is the more distant the enemy is, the more refinement is required of the sight alignment (particularly for slug use); conversely, the closer he is, the less precise your alignment must be (usually a glimpse of the front sight on the chest will do).

One key to the physical alignment necessary is the stock weld (also called a cheek weld). This is the consistent placement of the cheek on the comb of the stock. It must be placed on the same spot on the stock every time—on demand. Developing a consistent stock weld allows the master eye to look through the rear sight at the front sight the same way every time the shotgun is mounted into the shoulder (or at the front bead over the shotgun receiver). Extensive practice in shouldering the shotgun will ensure this.

The flash sight picture used in the snap shot involves the sharp shift of visual focus from the adversary (the source of the threat) to the front sight. This occurs as a sighting pause for an instant prior to shooting in order to verify that the physical alignment is correct.

This is the essence of the snap shot with a shotgun. Your eyes acquire the target, and you begin to move the gun into alignment with it. As the weapon's sights intercede into the line of sight, your support eye tracks the target as your dominant eye refines the sight picture as needed. This binocular function of the eyes, in conjunction with a solid gun mount, will get you on target quickly. Once on target, pause only long enough to verify correct alignment and break the shot.

Remember that the shotgun's spreading buckshot pattern allows a much wider margin for sight alignment error than will the use of a single projectile. Thus a buckshot-equipped shotgunner does not need to slow down as much as if slugs were in use. When the shotgun is loaded with slugs, the distances will likely exceed 20 to 25 yards, and the actual shot will be preceded by a longer time interval required by longer distances.

The flash sight picture concept works with all manner of sights, but it is most accurate with the ghost ring-type sights as mentioned in Chapter 5. This sight system allows the shooter to keep both his eyes open while focusing on the front sight. The rear sight becomes a softly focused ghost ring image to the shooter and enables extremely quick target acquisition.

The speed of the shot is dictated by two things: (1) the quickness of the mount (bringing the shotgun into a firing position), and (2) the quickness of sight recognition. A man with a quick mount and a quick eye can break an accurate shot in a hamster's heartbeat.

My old martial arts teacher was fond of saying, "Where the eyes go the mind follows, and where the mind goes the body follows." In tactical shooting, you might say that where the eyes go the attention follows, and where the attention goes the gun will follow. Not only must you visually identify the threat, you must also identify the exact spot on that threat that you wish to hit. The first thing you will probably notice is the adversary's hands. What those hands contain will determine your reaction. But after the threat has been realized, the eyes must move to the spot on that target that you want to hit (i.e., a point at the center of the target's mass). Ignoring this may cause you to align the shotgun on the adversary's hands instead. Think of this as looking at the threat through a telephoto lens instead of a wide angle. Instead of looking at the chest, look at the middle button of his shirt. This is not tunnel vision by any means: you still maintain your peripheral vision of what appears around you.

The way you look at possible adversaries must be developed and practiced just like your gunhandling skills. Eventually you will find yourself initially looking at the hands of everyone you come across and then subsequently shifting visual focus to the center of their chests. This is a good visual reflex to develop and cultivate.

The snap-shooting process as described in the text: one–two–three.

81

The mount into the shoulder and the stock weld must be instantaneous, smooth, and stripped of all unnecessary motions. This can only be accomplished through long, continuous, and proper training that programs the correct muscle memory for the gun mount into the subconscious mind. The result of this training is that we can think "go" and be right on target without consciously thinking out every step of the mount and shooting sequence.

After programming a solid gun mount and snap shot, you can begin to refine it with the eyes-off drill. This kinesthetic alignment drill has you visually acquire a dry-fire target (no ammunition needed here, boys) and mount the shotgun, noticing how perfect alignment feels. Now dismount the shotgun and maintain visual contact with the target. Close your eyes and, remembering the location of the target as well as how perfect alignment felt, quickly remount the shotgun. Dry-fire the shotgun and then open your eyes to verify your position. A master shotgunner will be able to execute this drill, open his eyes, and be aligned directly on target.

A second useful exercise is to mount the shotgun and, holding it on target, consciously and forcefully shift the visual focus from the target's hands to the target spot to the front sight. This develops a high degree of eye control. As you look at the target, you are still aware of the location of the front sight in relation to the target, although you may not be actively looking for it. Similarly, when you are looking at the front sight, you are still aware of the location of the target in your peripheral field.

Ideally, the shotgun mount and stock weld, the stopping of motion as the shotgun is aligned, the visual shift from target to front sight, and the firing of the snap shot will occur almost simultaneously. In ultraclose-quarters conflicts this is usually the case because you will be moving as fast as your body will allow. Here you must keep up with the action visually. You are not only shooting quickly, you are also looking quickly. If you maintain control of your eyes, you will probably maintain control of your shooting.

Using the flash sight picture and the snap shot in tactical situations is just as quick as any so-called instinct-shooting method. But the flash sight picture will allow you to hit what you need to hit. When the bullets fly, there is absolutely no room for error—even with a shotgun.

CHAPTER TEN

LOADING AND MAINTAINING CONTINUITY OF FIRE

"In every battle there comes a time when both sides consider themselves beaten. He who continues to attack wins."

—General George S. Patton, Requoted from *Cooper's Commentaries* by Jeff Cooper

While the majority of situations requiring shotgun fire are concluded with one or two shots, it is a wise operator who prepares for the time when more shots will be needed.

Loading modes for the shotgun may be broken down into three types: administrative loading, tactical reloading, and emergency reloading.

Administrative loading occurs under secure conditions prior to any sort of tactical contact or activity where such contact is expected. Administrative handling of the weapon should parallel tactical procedures as much as

85

possible in order to reinforce the necessary muscle memory as well as to minimize complexity.

When loading the shotgun, for example, you should hold the shotgun shell in the same manner as if loading it under fire. This method places the shotgun shell along the base of the four fingers to facilitate loading it into the weapon. Additionally, it is important to load the weapon with the support hand, since that is how you will reload in a fight. To further refine the tactical process and concept, I suggest loading the shotgun from the shell pouch on the belt (or on the gun) and then replacing the ammunition that has been loaded.

It is a good idea to carry the spare ammunition in the same location as a matter of habit and practice. This way when you need to reload, your hand will automatically reach for that location. I favor carrying my immediate reload on the belt in some sort of a two-shell belt pouch. Placing one shell holder on the right side of the belt buckle with two rounds of buckshot and another on the opposite side with two slugs serves me well. There are

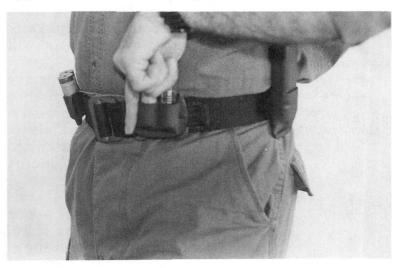

The shotgun shell belt pouch.

other methods, of course, such as butt cuffs and frame-mounted sidesaddle shell holders.

The administrative loading process that I recommend is as follows:

1. Hold the shotgun in the dominant hand (with the finger off the trigger and the muzzle in a safe direction).
2. Pull the fore-end back, thereby opening the bolt.
3. Retrieve a shell from the belt with the support hand.
4. Hold the shell at the base of the fingers and at a 90-degree angle to them (the hand position used to execute all of the loading functions.)
5. Bring the support hand under the receiver and against the open ejection port. It is now a simple matter to allow the round to drop into the ejection port.
6. Using the now empty support hand, close the bolt and chamber the round by running the fore-end forward. (If you do not wish to begin with a round in the chamber, you may delete the preceding steps.)

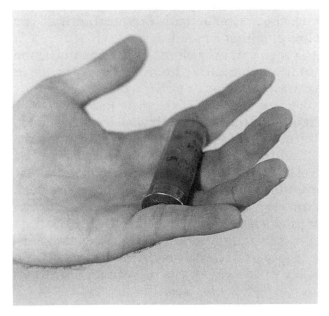

The "index" method of holding the shotgun shell.

87

If you wish only to load the magazine, do the following:

1. Hold the shotgun in the support hand with the bolt closed.
2. Retrieve a shell from the belt pouch and index it in the hand as described earlier.
3. Bring the shell under the receiver and at a point just forward of the trigger guard at the loading port.
4. Insert the shell forward into the tubular magazine, pushing it into place with your thumb.
5. Repeat the process as needed. You will now have a loaded magazine and, if you deleted the first instructions, an empty chamber.

If you want to chamber a round after loading the magazine, follow these steps:

1. Simply reach under the trigger guard with the dominant hand and activate the action-release lever. This will unlock the action and allow you to actuate the fore-end and chamber a round.
2. After doing this, you may wish to refill the magazine with an additional round or leave the empty space in the magazine.

The shotgun will now be in "tactical storage mode" (also called "cruiser ready"). This is the condition that a shotgun is in while in a police car or—in the case of a home-defense shotgun—in the closet. The magazine is loaded, the chamber is empty, and the hammer has been dropped on the empty chamber. Safety devices may be left on or off at the operator's discretion. The shotgun can be brought into action lickety-split from this condition, yet the empty chamber gives the operator a certain degree of safety in storage that a fully loaded shotgun might not.

As discussed earlier, *all guns are always loaded.* Sometimes you must check the status of a shotgun that you've been handed. To do so, simply activate the action release lever and retract the fore-end and bolt just enough to be able to look into the ejection port. If you see a shotgun shell, it is loaded. If your intention is to unload the piece, and yet you do not see a shell, you're advised to verify the empty chamber with a finger.

There are times when the shotgun must be unloaded completely and other times when just the chamber may need to be emptied (to download back into tactical storage). Again, keep the muzzle pointed in a safe direction. Actuate the action-release lever and move the fore-end to the rear far enough to begin ejecting the chambered round, yet not far enough to chamber the next round. Secure the chambered round as it emerges from the ejection port. Visually and physically check the chamber to ensure its unloaded status, and close the bolt by moving the fore-end forward. To place the weapon back into tactical storage, dry-fire the empty chamber and place the safety device in its desired position. The actual procedures will vary depending on the model of shotgun and its action, but the concepts remain the same.

Most often the problem will be handled with the ammunition that is in the gun (usually just a fraction of it). But like the opera that continues until the overweight maiden yodels, many a fight is not over when we think it is. A prudent operator always brings his weapon up to full capacity the first chance he gets. The dictum is *load what you shoot as soon as you can!* This means that if your single round has flattened a young urban terrorist bent on your demise, you should load another round into the magazine immediately during the "after-action" lull that may indicate the fight is over.

I've been in a few of these scrapes and can attest that every single one of them exhibited a tense pause at the perceived conclusion while everyone waited for the

On target, the shooter realizes that he should execute a tactical reload.

He reaches to the belt, retrieving one round.

He inserts the round into the magazine.

He pushes it all the way into the magazine. His eyes have not left the threat area during the process.

The shooter fires his last round and finds himself with an empty weapon in the middle of a fight.

He reaches to his belt and secures one round.

Indexing the round along the base of the four fingers, he pops it into the ejection port . . .

. . . and closes the bolt in order to chamber the round and is right back in the fight.

smoke to clear to see what happened. You can use that time to reload to full capacity in case you are wrong and the barbarians are just regrouping. It is at this time that it will occur to you that more ammunition may be required. Don't second guess your inner voice—*reload!*

The way we fulfill that need is the tactical reload. During the tactical reload there is no urgent need to keep shooting, but you keep the shotgun in a firing position— just in case. As in all nonshooting aspects of gunhandling, the trigger finger is *off* the trigger.

Secure the spare ammunition with the support hand and index the shotgun shell along the fingers. Bring the hand under the receiver and insert the shell into the load-

The Benelli Super 90's carrier-release button.

The Remington 11-87 carrier-release button.

ing port, pushing it into the magazine with the thumb. Repeat this as needed. As you can see, the only real difference between the tactical reload and the administrative load is your readiness and willingness to shoot.

Note that you can shoot at any time during the tactical reload. Since the tactical reload is a planned event, you will generally have ample time to get behind cover before commencing. You should never conduct a tactical reload in the kill zone if you can avoid it by getting behind something solid beforehand. The procedure is the same for any of the semiautomatic shotguns. On some of these (such as the Remington 11-87 or the Benelli Super 90), the carrier-release button must be activated.

Other times, the notion of reloading will not occur to you until you realize that your weapon is empty, and yet the problem of decking your adversaries hasn't been solved. What will happen is that when you try to shoot at a hostile, your gun will either give you the classic click in lieu of a bang, or your semiautomatic's bolt will have locked open on an empty chamber. That is the stimulus that must trigger your emergency reload procedure. Also, the way that the action cycles (in the case of a slide-action shotgun) will sometimes feel different if a cartridge has not been fed into the chamber. If you detect such a situation before having to fire, rectify it immediately by reloading. In such cases, there will probably be a pressing need to keep shooting the hostiles in front of you. This is a bad situation, but it can be solved with prior planning.

The fastest solution is simply to grab the pistol on your hip and keep shooting. The shotgun may be set aside with the support hand while the dominant hand draws and fires the pistol. If the shotgun is equipped with a tactical sling, you may simply drop it and let it hang as both hands obtain the pistol and you return fire. If the situation has really gotten bad and your relatives are already lining up to collect your pension

93

An alternate method for staying in the fight is to transfer from the shotgun to the pistol.

checks, simply discard the empty shotgun and stay in the fight with the pistol. This is an important skill to practice and develop into a conditioned reflex, along with your movement to cover.

What's that? You don't have your pistol with you? Bad show. The next best thing is to perform an emergency reload on the shotgun. As with the tactical reload, it is wise to seek cover before reloading. If you are practiced enough, you will be able to move to cover *as* you reload the shotgun.

When using a slide-action shotgun, keep in mind that you train to pump the action as a secondary motor skill automatically after pressing the trigger and in conjunction with the recoil. This means that even if you mentally realize that your final shot has been fired (a truly unlikely event), you will reflexively begin to pump the action to the rear. Even if you press the trigger and produce a click, your ingrained reflex will be to begin pulling the fore-end to the rear (secondary motor reflex). When you decide to reload, the bolt will probably be to the rear. This being the case, secure a shell with the support hand and hold it along the base of the four fingers as you always do while reloading. Bring the palm under the receiver and index the heel of the palm at the bottom of the receiver. This will automatically place your hand in a position to drop the fresh shell into the ejection port. After you drop the round in, a simple forward motion of the fore-end will chamber it and get you back into the fight.

The semiautomatic shotguns will generally lock the bolt back on an empty chamber, and the procedure is the same. You must depress the carrier release to release the bolt and load the round into the chamber.

If your semiautomatic does not lock back on an empty chamber, you must load into the loading port as in the tactical reload and then cycle the action to chamber the round.

There are some specially made tubes available that

will allow an operator to speed load a completely emptied shotgun. The problem with these is that they are cumbersome and unreliable. Additionally, the tactical need to fully load an empty shotgun in a firefight is a fanciful notion. Better to simply use the methods described herein and eschew gadgetry. These things are neat toys for game shooting, but they have no tactical value whatsoever: avoid them.

The administrative reload is a preparatory loading procedure. The tactical reload is a planned procedure that is executed during a lull in the fight that might signify the conclusion of hostilities. The emergency reload is a reactive, exigent procedure that is executed during a fight because the tempo of the confrontation has escalated beyond your ability to manage your ammunition. The emergency reload must be a conditioned response to the stimulus of suddenly having an empty shotgun. Keep this in mind when you face the barbarians . . . and may you never run dry!

CHAPTER ELEVEN

DEVELOPING REACTIVE SHOOTING SKILLS

"You never have trouble if you are prepared for it."

—Theodore Roosevelt,
Roosevelt in the Badlands

The first concern in becoming proficient in tactical shooting is the development of a combat mind-set. This will keep you alert and let you know when it is time to fight. Once you understand that concept, you must develop realistic fighting techniques into conditioned reflexes and then refine those reflexes by extensive use of reactive shooting drills.

The type of shooting required in an actual gunfight involves the interaction between the shooter and the target (i.e., the officer and suspect, or the homeowner and the intruder). This interaction

97

deals with the actions, reactions, and perceptions of both parties. The rules of engagement in our free society indicate that we must generally allow the aggressor to initiate the confrontation. Subsequently, you will be reacting to the threatening actions of the adversary. When you recognize that your suspicions of pending combat are quite real, you will probably be in an active and agitated mental state. A complete training program must produce a certain amount of agitation to get you accustomed to reacting under stress. Such agitation may be artificially induced to a certain degree by the challenge produced by introducing short reaction time intervals as well as using targets that require you to *think* before and after shooting.

Reactive shooting also demands reflexive motor skills (i.e., all gunhandling and gun operations) because your thought processes will be tied up in locating, evaluating, and reacting to the adversaries threatening you. If you must actually stop to think about how to execute a reload, or how you want your sight picture to look, you will fall behind and die. The reactive training program emphasizes managing the weapon by reflex so that the conscious mind will be free to deal with the immediate environment.

Visual skills are as important as shooting skills. In a gunfight, you use the eyes dynamically to scan for and locate the adversary. When this is done, you also scan the adversary to determine the level of threat, paying particular attention to his hands. You might shift the visual focus from the target to the front sight back and forth several times during the confrontation while the decision to shoot or not is pending. A reactive-shooting program must address the development of these visual skills as well as the more traditional shooting techniques.

An adversary may only expose himself to your gunfire for a brief moment before disappearing behind cover or shooting at you. You must conduct your tactical training in a manner that reflects extremely small time

98

frames to react to and subsequently shoot a target. These "reaction windows" must be within your realistic capability, but they must also be a challenge.

Such concerns may be addressed by keeping the targets in a dark environment and having a training partner suddenly light them up for you to see or by facing away from the targets while your partner sets them up and then executing a 180-degree pivot on command prior to engaging them. Limiting the exposure time will force you to begin developing reactive and reflexive shooting skills.

Recognizing that the fight is over is just as important as knowing it has begun, particularly in our ridiculously litigious era. Traditional shotgun training programs have you shoot a predetermined number of shots or shoot until the weapon is empty.

In a real confrontation, you must react quickly and violently to a threat, but you must also stop shooting when that threat has been neutralized (the suspect is down). Your training must provide some sort of visual clue that your gunfire has been successful and that further shooting is not required.

Such reactive and interactive training cannot be thrust upon someone without sufficient preparation. Doing so is like expecting a recent graduate of high school driver's training to compete in the Indy 500! Reactive-shooting training must be approached in a goal-directed, building-block manner where one drill leads to the next one.

The first order of business is to get you accustomed to looking at the target and assessing whether it is a threat. With a shotgun, you are often limited to using steel targets by simple economics (at least in the beginning). Buckshot destroys paper too easily. A few steel targets of suitable shape and size will be of immense help and last almost forever.

I've found that the best tool for developing this skill quickly is the color-shape drill. Construct a cardboard stencil depicting four shapes. I've used a square, a circle, a diamond, and a triangle. Next, spray paint these shapes with a stencil onto a steel target. It is helpful to use four different colors for the four shapes (such as red, blue, green, and black) and to avoid repeating a color-shape combination on the target array. Using four targets, four shapes, and four colors, you can come up with an astonishing variety of combinations.

To execute the drill, stand facing the target array about 7 yards away, with the shotgun in the prescribed ready position. Your training partner—standing behind you—will call out either a color, or a shape, or a combination of both (e.g., red, square, or red square). When you hear his command, rapidly scan the target array for the shape or color in question. When you locate it, shoot it and knock down the steel target depicting it. The color-shape combination may appear on more than one target. If so, you must engage them all. If the color-shape combination does not appear at all in the target array, you have a nonshooting situation. This exercise begins to make you *think* before you shoot and to take the "shooting cue" from what you *perceive* of the targets.

The preceding drill teaches you to look at the targets and to scan them for an indication of threat before engaging. The colors and shapes are easy to distinguish from the plain background so it is easy to receive instant verification of the decision to shoot at a particular target.

The next step is to refine the process further by training yourself to look at the hands for an indication of threat. Replace the color-shape targets with two stenciled human hands for each target. These hands may be left "empty," or you may add overlays depicting guns or other weapons. Have a training partner set them up for you so you don't know which ones to shoot. The actual implementation of this exercise doesn't change, except that you will now be looking specifically at the hands. The "order of battle" is simple: any adversary with a weapon is to be considered a threat and subsequently shot.

The entire target is no longer festooned with colors or shapes as it was before, so you will find yourself looking directly at the hands with a sort of condensed visual focus. You must now learn to shift the visual focus from the hands as soon as the threat is perceived. The reason for this visual shift is that you will move the shotgun toward whatever your eyes are looking at; after all, you do not want to shoot him in the hands. Shift your visual focus to the center of mass of the target and, invariably, that is where the shotgun will go. This will reinforce the concept of the flash sight picture. Your hits will quickly verify the location of your visual focus on the target before your eyes come back in to the front sight.

Shooting targets at such close range, and with a shotgun no less, will not require the precise sight alignment of the medium-range slug shooter or rifleman, but some sort of sight picture must still be seen. This drill teaches you to shift visual focus from the hands to the vital zone as the shotgun is brought up into shooting position. You will index your shotgun reflexively toward what you are viewing. As the shotgun's sights intersect the line of sight, you must glimpse the sight picture and take particular note of the location of the front sight as the shot is fired. The appearance of the flash sight picture dictates the speed of the shot. A relatively aligned sight picture represents a relatively aligned shotgun, and a verification that everything is correct before firing.

The stenciled hands on the targets stand out like the proverbial sore thumbs and are quite easily seen and recognized. The next evolution uses any of the humanoid photograph targets depicting actual people. These targets are much more difficult to scan and evaluate because of their greater detail. Additionally, the hands do not seem to stand out as they did with the previous drill, and you must actively look for them. These targets are not very

101

resilient to shotgun fire and must be replaced after almost every shot, but their training value more than makes up for this. Again, have your training partner set them up without your knowledge to attain full training value.

These picture targets may be "armed" with a variety of items, ranging from knives, guns, and sawed-off shotguns to broken bottles. Bystander targets may be equipped with cameras, newspapers, badges, and even video cameras (don't shoot these). This drill is also useful for introducing "target triage." Here you must determine the level of threat among several threat cues and the subsequent order of response to them. The targets may be arranged close and distant, as well as with a variety of contact weapons or firearms. You must not only determine which one is a friend and which a foe, you must also prioritize the order in which you will respond based on the proximity and capability of the threat. For example, a man with a knife at arm's length is a much more immediate threat than a man with a pistol across the street.

It is important that you not see the target array prior to engaging to avoid any actual planning on your part. Don't be a gamesman and try to cheat—you will only be cheating yourself.

The three prior drills emphasized taking your cue to start shooting from what you see in the target's hands as a threat or nonthreat. You learned to "triage" the targets according to threat level and proximity of threat and to use the flash sight picture for ensuring hits. Now you must learn when to stop shooting, and the targets are the medium for this as well.

In a gunfight, you must keep shooting until the threat has stopped—usually when the suspect goes down. You react to your adversary's reaction to your gunfire. The training environment must provide that stimulus as well. If the target is still standing, you must keep shooting. If the target goes down, you stop shooting—hold your fire and cover it, ready to shoot again.

There are several sophisticated computerized systems that allow shooting at a video screen with laser-equipped weapons. These have some training value but are expensive enough to be out of the financial reach of most individual users and many small police agencies. The sophistication of the training facilities are only limited by finances. But do not despair if your wallet looks as empty as a liberal politician's word of honor. With some ingenuity, a functional and fully reactive range may be set up for a minor expense.

Knock-down reactive targets have been around for many years. The most prevalent of these are the "pepper-popper" type, although they are now also available in a more humanoid form. These targets are designed to fall down when they are hit solidly by a pistol round. They also work very well for shotgun reactive training. They work even better for developing reactive shooting skills when a standard photographic target is affixed to its surface with tape.

Now when we hit the target solidly, there will be an instant reaction: it will fall back. When it does, regardless of how many rounds this requires, we will program the need to stop shooting based on the target's actions. Such a reactive target can also teach the value of the failure-to-stop technique, or "shotgun Mozambique." As I've already mentioned, the best solution to an adversary that is not suitably impressed with your choice in buckshot (that must be *some* adversary, eh?) is a shot to the cranial area. These steel targets come in a variety of shapes and sizes and may be set up so that only a head shot will bring them down. With pistol training, it is a simple matter to calibrate the targets for the desired effect. When it comes to shotguns, the way to do this is to use a smaller target approximately the size of the target's head resembling a lollipop. Attach the head portion of the paper target to the small target and you are ready to go. Shots to the body area will not knock it down

103

because there is no target metal there to take the hit and cause the target to fall. One to the body and then, if no reaction, a head shot. The point is that you don't know a head shot will be required until the target doesn't go down and *then* you must react to it.

Those on tough shooting budgets (who isn't?) who cannot afford to purchase metal targets can experience the same level of training by using balloons. The balloons may be tied to overhead supports in an indoor range, or be supported from below in the great outdoors. The cardboard-backed photographic targets may now be taped to the balloons so that their placement coincides with the vital zone of the targets. When the target is shot correctly, the balloon blows up and the now unsupported target falls. It is important here to remain watchful for a good pattern on the actual target since the balloon may be "taken out" by a single pellet.

Such reactive targets are perfect for use in tactical simulators or "kill houses" that require moving through an area (indoor or outdoor) hunting for hostile targets. This type of training begins to blend tactical thinking with tactical movement, as well as the previously developed skills. In this training environment, you may be faced with an unknown threat that does not warrant gunfire but may, nevertheless, be hostile. Such targets may be ordered to get down and captured from behind cover without resorting to gunfire. Or they may show their intent from the outset and require immediate termination. This again instills the reflex of looking before shooting.

The final drill for reactive shooting is the force-on-force simulation. This simulation is akin to the role-playing that police recruits learn in the academy. The only difference is that if you foul up, you really get shot—shot with Simmunition FX Special Effects Marking Cartridges, that is. These FX cartridges are water-soluble paint pellets loaded into proprietary brass cases. These FX cartridges fire from the trainee's own weapon with a simple and inexpensive user-installed kit. The cartridges themselves were originally intended for pistols and submachine guns, but they've recently produced a conversion kit for use in shotguns. The kit includes 12-gauge shotshell-type cartridge adapters into which the .38-.357 FX cartridges can be inserted. These will not function in a semiautomatic, but they work nicely in a slide-action. Center-of-mass accuracy can be achieved within and up to about 30 feet, but good hits may still be obtained at distances well beyond that (quite a long way in a gunfight). The safety-conversion kit also contains a barrel insert that precludes the inadvertent chambering or firing of any live ammunition in the training scenario. FX cartridges allow the trainee to hunt for, locate, assess, and react to the most realistic "target" that he will ever face—another human being who does not want to get shot and who will do his best to shoot back. The bright, visible paint hits show unarguable outcomes and, at 400 fps, sting enough to provide a real incentive to use careful tactics.

These FX cartridges come with comprehensive safety instructions that stress the use of face and eye protection and discourage any shots to exposed skin areas. The FX cartridges cannot be beat for realism in training. To borrow the old ad line, I can say without hesitation that "it's the next best thing to being there."

The initial training received by a combatant must encompass the basics of marksmanship, reflexive gun-handling, and the combat mind-set. But when these are well ingrained, you must strive to develop your reactive shooting skills. The first steps in this endeavor are to use the assessment of the target to determine the tactical response. (To shoot or not to shoot? That is the question.) Later, attempt to interject variables to stimulate judgment under duress. You will learn to determine order of threat and target triage based on proximity and immediacy of threats. The next level introduces reactive targets and the recognition of when to stop shooting based on the target's reaction, as well as the shotgun Mozambique drill. These are then brought together in tactical simulations where tactical thinking and dynamic shooting skills work together to contact and either neutralize or capture targets. The final level is that of force-on-force simulation through the use of FX paint-marking cartridges.

The combat shooting world has indeed made great advancements in the past few years, but that advancement must not be halted. The training we undergo must simulate the characteristics of real-world confrontations as closely as safety will allow. After a strong foundation in the basics, regular training in reactive and interactive shooting skills will go far in doing just that. Regarding training, as General Patton once said, "a pint of sweat will save a gallon of blood." Amen!

CHAPTER TWELVE

THE SWITCH-TO-SLUG DRILL

"The man who knows he can shoot and hit will get himself out of a bad spot."

—H.W. McBride,
A Rifleman Went to War

The theoretical possibility of being able to switch to a different type of ammunition (usually a slug) is one of the greatest advantages of the shotgun in many users' minds. The practical reality of accomplishing this maneuver is dependent on several things.

First is the availability of rifled slugs on scene. Clearly, you cannot switch to what you do not have. Many shotgunners, by department policy, are not equipped with shotgun slugs. Sometimes the slugs are simply left behind when the buckshot-equipped shotgun is grabbed.

Second is the establish-

107

The author takes aim at a distant target with a slug-loaded shotgun.

ment of a drill to quickly and efficiently execute the switch to slug. The switch to slug is a reactive technique that you execute in response to a perception that buckshot will no longer suffice. This drill must be ingrained in the motor reflexes so that when you perceive the need, there will be no delay in its execution.

Third, the circumstances when you would execute the switch to slug must be thought out before they occur. In a gunfight, the tempo of events will often surpass your ability to keep up, mentally speaking. You will rely on your trained reactions to the rapidly incoming stimulus. If you perceive a stimulus whose appropriate response is a switch to slugs (just as a click instead of a bang is the stimulus to reload), your response will be instantaneous.

With these things in mind, you must ask when would such a switch be appropriate and why. A slug will be the answer whenever you see a hostile target beyond the limit of the B Zone (about 20 yards). Additionally, a slug is the way to go if a greater degree of precision or

108

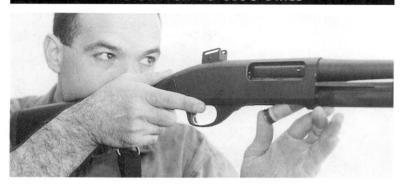

The switch-to-slug drill involves selecting a slug load from the belt (or other carry position) and inserting it into the magazine.

The support hand actuates the fore-end pump, thereby ejecting the chambered round and chambering a slug load.

109

The dominant hand activates the action-release lever.

penetration is desired (e.g., an impromptu hostage rescue or a hostile behind light cover).

Switching to the slug will require several seconds. This may be longer than is available in a rapidly evolving confrontation. Then again, distant adversaries allow you greater time to deal with them. Similarly, with the dreaded hostage scenario, you will rarely require an instant shot with a shotgun. This means that you will generally have a reasonable amount of time to select the slug as well as adopt some sort of supported position behind cover. As with the reloading drills, adopting a covered position must become an integral part of the switch-to-slug drill.

The recognition of the need for a slug must be accompanied by a simultaneous move toward cover as the slug is secured (if cover is available). The shotgunner will see his adversary (or target) and realize that buckshot will not *reach* or *penetrate*. The next step is to secure the slug with the support hand and adopt a supported position (behind cover if possible). It is very important to *carry the slugs in the same place every time* so that you will know where they are located immediately. Additionally, keep them in a separate location from your buckshot.

110

The action-release lever on a Smith & Wesson 3000 shotgun. The action-release lever is in the same place for the Remington 870 shotgun.

This way you will know reflexively where to reach for a particular type of ammunition. Having to search your pockets for those precious slugs while bullets whiz past your ears in effect invalidates the whole concept. Also, it is important to recognize ammunition types by touch. A slug will have the slug tip exposed, whereas a buckshot round will have the crimp at the tip.

The procedure for a slide-action shotgun is as follows. Keep the shotgun oriented to the target while the dominant hand maintains its hold on the pistol grip of the stock. Bring the slug under the receiver and insert it into the loading port. With the dominant hand, reach under the receiver and activate the action release as the support hand actuates the fore-end, thereby ejecting the chambered buckshot round and chambering the slug.

For the Remington 1100/1187 family of semiautomatics, the procedure is similar. The only difference is that you have no slide action to pump. Instead, use the support hand: move it from its usual position on the fore-end, in a clockwise sweep, to catch the bolt handle and operate the bolt. This in turn will eject the buckshot round and chamber the slug.

The drill is much different for the Benelli Super 90. If

The switch-to-slug drill for the Remington 11-87 as demonstrated by Officer Richard Camacho. First, secure a slug from the belt (or vest).

Insert it into the magazine.

Cycle the bolt to eject and feed.

Back in action.

The Remington 11-87.

113

The procedure for the Benelli shotgun as demonstrated by Officer Eric Uyeno. First secure the slug load.

Next, pull back the bolt with the dominant hand while supporting the shotgun with the support hand (while holding the slug load).

the Super 90's bolt is manually operated, the hammer will be cocked, but a cartridge will not feed from the magazine unless the latch provided alongside the receiver is depressed. The procedure for the Super 90 is to bring the slug under the receiver as in the emergency reload procedure. Next, bring the slug alongside the ejection port. Now, support the shouldered gun on the web of the support hand between thumb and index finger. Pull back

114

Insert the slug load into the chamber . . .

. . . and activate the carrier-release button.

Ready to go!

115

The Benelli Super 90 M3 may also be operated as a pump-action shotgun.

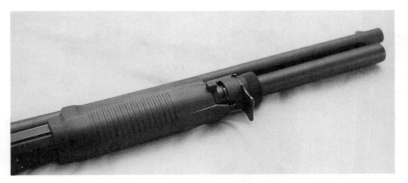

The lever at the extreme forward end of the fore-end allows the shotgun to be a semiautomatic or a pump-action.

the bolt with the dominant hand and hold it in the fully retracted position. This will eject the chambered buck-shot round. Now, drop the slug into the ejection port, release the bolt, and you are ready to shoot.

It is important to develop the switch-to-slug drill as a reaction to a stimulus that has been presented to the shooter. During training, include some sort of decision-making process for the selection of slugs. A predeter-mined situation (whose solution is the slug selection) must be suddenly presented during a firing drill. A quick switch-to-slug response to this stimulus will reinforce the mental process you wish to develop.

Whether the switch-to-slug drill is a viable tactical option or only a theoretical possibility remains to be answered. A police officer I know once executed this drill under fire, but his fleeing adversaries were no longer legally requiring gunfire. Training to develop this skill like you wish to use it in a fight will allow you to respond properly when things don't go as planned.

CHAPTER THIRTEEN

SUPPORTED POSITIONS WITH THE SHOTGUN

"In the final result, it does not matter how brave a man is, but how closely he can hold."
—S.E. White,
Requoted from *Gargantuan Gunsite Gossip* by Jeff Cooper

Shooting a slug-loaded shotgun is similar to shooting a rifle. One of the caveats of the rifleman is to get as steady as the circumstances will allow before actually shooting. Keeping true to that rule, the study of supported positions is a fundamental staple of the rifleman, as well as the slug-equipped shotgunner. It is also useful to know and be proficient in the use of these shooting positions to use any available cover to its fullest potential. In fact, after you develop a good understanding of these positions, it is important to include the assumption of cover along

119

Whenever possible, try to match the position chosen to the cover available.

Assuming the prone position. Pivot on the dominant-side ball of the foot toward the strong side (about 45 degrees).

Drop down to the knees in the direction of your pivot.

Above Left: Release the grip on the weapon with the dominant-side hand and catch your fall as you lean forward.

Above: Lower your support-side elbow down on the deck, keeping the shotgun barrel pointed toward the target.

Left: Regrip the shotgun "pistol grip" with your dominant hand and pull the weapon's butt into the shoulder.

with the practice of the actual shooting positions themselves. For simplicity of discussion, we will begin all position assumptions from a high-ready carry position facing the target, but they may be assumed from any carry mode.

Generally, the lower your position is to the deck, the more accurately you will be able to place your shots. To accomplish this, ideally you shoot from the prone position, which allows you to use extremely low cover that would preclude the use of a higher profile shooting position.

To assume the prone position with a shotgun, pivot on the dominant-side ball of the foot toward the strong side (about 45 degrees). Drop down to the knees in the direction of your pivot. Release the grip on the weapon with the dominant-side hand and catch your fall as you lean forward. Let your support-side elbow down on the deck, keeping the shotgun barrel pointed toward the target. It is important to note that your body is moving at an angle toward the target, but your visual focus as well as weapon orientation is directly toward the target or threat. Regrip the shotgun "pistol grip" with your dominant hand and pull the weapon's butt into the shoulder. Your body should be at about a 35-to-45-degree angle in relation to the target. Your feet should be comfortably placed apart with the insides of the ankles flat on the deck. Be careful that no portion of your body is exposed when practicing with cover. It is imperative to maintain the support elbow directly under the gun to avoid lateral dispersion of your shots.

Here are some notes on the shotgun prone position you should remember. Shooting a semiautomatic shotgun from prone is easy. It is when pump-actions enter the picture that everyone gets nervous about shooting from prone. Pumping the fore-end from the prone position is not difficult. Simply roll toward the dominant side far enough to ease the weight on the support-side elbow. This may tend to cant the shotgun slightly

Activating a pump-action shotgun from the prone position is easy.

toward the dominant side. Now you can pump the action as usual. Also practice reloading from prone to ensure that whatever method you use for extra ammunition (or alternate ammunition) will still work when you are flat on your belly.

Be careful about how you get into the prone position. I have seen action bar locks on pump-action guns sheared off as a result of vigorous assumption of prone positions—butt first. This either completely jammed the shotgun for any follow-up shots or it disabled the safety factor of locking the action prior to shooting. In any case, when going prone, avoid contacting the ground with your butt —your shotgun butt, that is.

Understand also that moving out of a prone position does not happen in a jiffy. Getting up and getting out of that position and location will be substantially slower than from many other supported positions, so avoid it if the adversary is closer that 100 yards.

The next level in ascending height is the squatting position. The squat is useful for circumstances where cover is about waist high and a quick change of location may be necessary. This is also quite useful in areas where such debris on the ground as broken glass or building rubble will prevent assumption of any lower positions.

123

Above: Pivot toward the dominant side on the balls of your feet as you maintain visual focus on the threat.

Above Right: Lower your body until your buttocks rest on your calves, with both feet flat on the floor.

Right: Both elbows extend well past the knees with the backs of the arms resting on the knees.

Again, just as in the assumption of the prone position, you pivot toward the dominant side on the balls of your feet as you maintain visual focus on the threat. Now, simply lower your body until your buttocks rest on your calves. Both feet must be flat on the deck for this position to be stable. Both elbows extend well past the knees with the backs of the arms resting on the knees.

Kneeling is as useful as squatting and generally fits the same circumstances. Kneeling is a better choice if the operator's physical capabilities don't allow squatting. One advantage of both kneeling and squatting is that they lower the gun mount (body) and allow you to elevate the line of fire. This is useful for shooting upward into a close adversary to minimize overpenetration.

To assume a kneeling position, pivot on the ball of the dominant-side foot so that it now points 90 degrees from the target. Step across an imaginary line projecting from the dominant-side foot toward the target with the support-side foot. Now, as the weapon is brought into

Shooting a distant target from the kneeling position.

Above: Assuming a kneeling position. Pivot on the ball of the dominant-side foot so that it now points 90 degrees from the target.

Above Right: Step across an imaginary line projecting from the dominant-side foot toward the target with the support-side foot.

Right: As the weapon is brought into the shoulder, simply sit down on the dominant-side foot.

the shoulder, you simply sit down on the dominant-side foot. Place the back of the support-side arm on the flat portion of the knee. Again, keep the support-side elbow vertical to maintain lateral stability. The strength of these positions is enhanced by a slight forward lean to counteract the recoiling forces of the shotgun. Note that when the adversary is close and only coarse shooting is needed, there is no need to support the elbow(s), and a standard upper body shooting position will do.

As much as you try to keep the shotgun steady, realize that you cannot keep it from moving completely. What you can do, however, is strive constantly to keep the sights aligned with each other and with the place you want to hit. Movement of the front sight within the aperture rear sight (ghost ring) represents changing angles of the shotgun barrel. Changing this angle of the barrel relative to the target represents a miss with a slug. The more distant the target, the more precise that angle must be within the capabilities of your ammunition. If your front sight is perfectly aligned within the rear aperture, the shotgun can move a considerable amount and still be on target. In theory, your perfectly centered front sight can move within a 10-inch circle, and you'll still be able to fire a 10-inch group with slugs way out there across the

Use whatever support is available if shooting beyond 50 yards.

canyon. But you must hold that alignment before, during, and after the shot. The same is true for bead-sighted guns, albeit with somewhat reduced accuracy potential.

The realities of requiring a shot at the length of a football field are slim for anyone who has properly studied his "opponent" (i.e., select a rifle to solve likely rifle problems), but you do not want to limit your capabilities in the event that your studies were not complete. In such cases, the availability of slugs and an understanding of supported shooting positions will allow you to reach out and . . . well, you know.

CHAPTER FOURTEEN

HANDLING MALFUNCTIONS

*"Weapons should be hardy
rather than decorative."*
—Miyamoto Musashi,
The Book of Five Rings

One fact of life remains constant regardless of the efficiency of your weapons: anything that is man-made can malfunction or break. This is no less true in the field of combat weapons. The worst of it is that this usually occurs when it is least expected or desired.

It is important to realize the difference between a simple malfunction or stoppage and a broken weapon. A malfunction may be easily cleared with the appropriate maneuver, and the weapon can be brought back into the fight in the blink of an eye. A broken or jammed weapon requires the services of

129

an armorer to fix and is of little more tactical use than a baseball bat. Neither one of these situations is predictive of lasting health and well-being when the criminals are shooting at you.

Some malfunctions are easily cleared, while others are often accompanied by great consternation and muffled profanities. The best solution, of course, is to maintain the weapon and its ammunition in proper working order and avoid the problem completely.

Malfunctions are often caused by obviously worn or damaged ammunition or by abused weapons. I can't begin to recall how often I've found cartridges with worn-out case rims (from repeated chambering and downloading) or cartridges with misshapen shell walls from being subjected to excessive heat day after day inside of a locked police vehicle. I've also found rusted and nearly inoperative shotguns neglected in a vehicle's trunk after some long-forgotten seaside surveillance. These things can all be "fixed" before the moment of truth. All you have to do is check.

Even if you keep your weapons in pristine condition, there is a chance that they will not serve you best when the time demands it. The best preparation for such eventualities is stimulus-response training. This form of training inculcates a specific response (malfunction-clearing drill) as an answer to a given stimulus (gun doesn't shoot). Your ability to read and recognize the stimulus will facilitate a quick, efficient, and immediate response.

The quickest and simplest malfunction drill for the shotgun is to secure or ground the shotgun and produce the pistol to solve the disagreement. If transition to a second weapon is not an option, you must clear the stoppage and get back into the fight.

The first malfunction we will discuss is the failure to fire, aka position-one stoppage. You know that you have a position-one stoppage if you hear a click instead of a

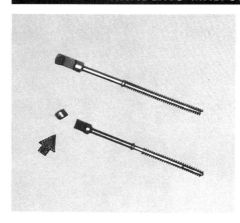

A broken firing pin can ruin your whole day.

bang. The immediate solution must be a vigorous cycling of the action through the fore-end pump, or the bolt handle in a semiautomatic shotgun. This will eject the unfired dud and reload with a fresh cartridge. If you hear a second click after the attempted clearing drill, it may mean that you have

For a failure to fire, first pump the action to the rear and simultaneously flip the weapon to the right. Close the bolt (chambering a fresh round) and get back in the fight.

If a shell gets caught in the action and cannot be ejected, creating a feedway stoppage, drop to the kneeling position and slam the butt on the deck as you pump the action back.

This should clear the problem. From the kneeling position, come up sharply into the underarm assault position.

a broken firing pin (or other broken part). A failure to fire is caused by either a bad primer or broken firing pin. It may also be caused by operator error in the form of "short-stroking," or partial cycling. Remember to operate the pump briskly and vigorously every time you fire to ensure ejection prior to feeding.

The second malfunction is the failure to eject, aka position-two stoppage. The stimulus for this situation is the realization that the expended shell has not been ejected and is either trapped in the ejection port or protruding from it. Additional clues will probably include an inoperative trigger and an out-of-battery bolt with the semiautomatic. With the pump-action you will be unable to close the fore-end pump because of the offending shell.

The solution is to pull the fore-end (and bolt) back sharply while simultaneously flipping the weapon to the right (ejection port down). This will usually clear out the problem and get you back into action.

Position-two stoppages are caused by cartridges with damaged case rims or by worn extractors and ejectors.

The third type of malfunction is the feedway stoppage, or position-three stoppage. The circumstances and solutions for manual and semiauto shotguns differ markedly so we will discuss each one individually.

Sometimes a shell in the magazine of a pump shotgun will jump past the latch that holds it in place. This in effect ties up the action and prevents the fore-end from being cycled.

The solution for a pump action is to kneel or squat down and slam the shotgun butt on the deck as you attempt to cycle the action to eject the spent shell and chamber a fresh cartridge. Make no mistake, this is *very* hard on the gun. Damaging a shotgun in order to win a gunfight is an acceptable loss, but damaging one every week in practice is not.

The principle is the same for the semiautomatic shotgun. This time you must actuate the bolt, via the bolt lever, while conducting the same operation. A similar malfunction might be caused by an overexpanded shell in the chamber. The same fix applies.

The first line of defense is a properly maintained weapon. Next, you need fresh ammunition that does not show signs of neglect or overuse. Last, in case your preparations did not ward off the Murphy family, you need a planned immediate response to unexpected malfunctions.

CHAPTER FIFTEEN

DEALING WITH MULTIPLE ADVERSARIES

"You must drive the enemy together as if tying a line of fishes, and when they seem to be piled up, cut them down strongly without giving them room to move."

—Miyamoto Musashi,
The Book of Five Rings

The trends and patterns of urban gunfights indicate that it is quite likely that you will face more than one adversary. When this happens, your exposure to danger rises drastically. If luck is with you and you've been alert, you'll receive prior warning to the situation and conduct a tactical escape. If escape is not possible or desirable, at least you'll get behind cover before the festivities start and conduct an unexpected counterattack of your own. Whatever the outcome, standing around undecided until you are looking down their muzzles is a foolish thing to do.

135

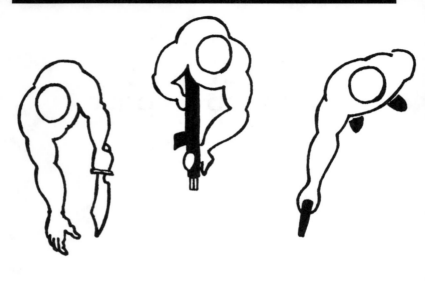

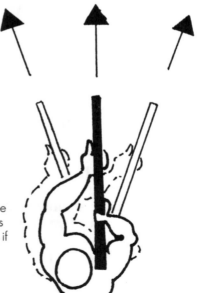

Dealing with three hostiles at once is risky—especially if they are all in a position to shoot at you.

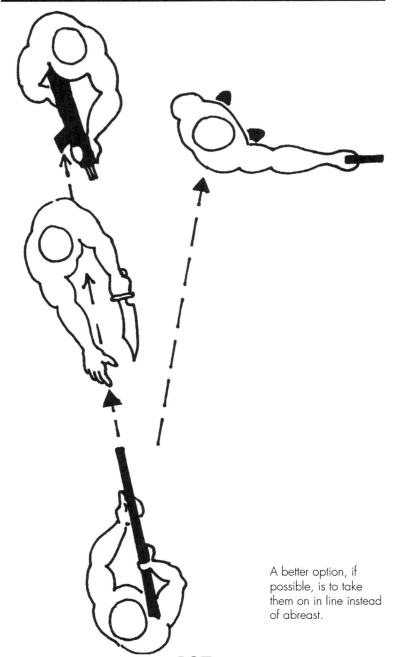

A better option, if possible, is to take them on in line instead of abreast.

137

During the preconfrontation phase, if tactical escape is not an option, you must look for something to use as cover. Ideally, your position will place you in an enfilade with the hostiles; that means you will be able to fire at them along a linear axis (lengthwise) rather than across their line if they were standing abreast.

It is important to first shoot the man who is the most immediate threat to you. Assuming that all the hostiles are armed, the one whose attention is focused on you will generally be the most immediate threat. This does not always mean the one with the most powerful weapon or the one closest to you. You must shoot the man who is most capable of killing you in your present position first and then proceed in a descending order of threat.

When there is more than one hostile shooting at you, their chances of hitting you increases in proportion to their number. Therefore, it is imperative to get behind something solid as soon as you can. If you are already under fire, you must deal with the problem with sudden extreme violence before moving to cover or, better yet, shoot on the move as you escape to cover.

If the cover you've chosen only shields you from some of the adversaries, you must shoot the ones you're exposed to first. There is no place for discussions or bargaining here. Once the fight has begun, you'd better keep shooting until they all the hostiles are down or until they break off their attack and you can escape.

You must develop the ability to roll out from behind cover in a shooting position behind your gun muzzle without overexposing yourself to gunfire or allowing your barrel to protrude beyond cover. Be aware that if your feet are exposed underneath your cover, your adversaries' projectiles may accidentally (or intentionally) skip along the deck and strike your feet. You may be able to use this tactic to your benefit as well.

When dealing with a single opponent, you can afford to hammer him into submission if that is necessary. You don't have that option when facing a group. Other than to shoot the most immediate threat first, it is vital to get a hit on each man once and to do so quickly. You must shoot each man once and move on to the next one, picking up any remaining hostiles afterward. You do not want to pummel one particular man with an entire magazine of ammunition and ignore his two friends (who are also shooting at you). You must evaluate as you shoot—that is, you let your eyes come off the sights and travel downrange to evaluate the results of your shooting after one sweep. Keep the shotgun pointed at them in the event that more shots are required.

If possible, try to shoot from the dominant side toward the support side. It is substantially easier to track with the gun muzzle a target that is toward the support side. Conversely, it is more difficult to do so with a target that is toward the dominant side. Additionally, shooting toward the support side is more efficient physically than toward the opposite because it follows the natural range of movement of the body. This does not preclude shooting the most immediate threat first, since that may dictate the travel path of your gun muzzle. It is best, of course, to be practiced in both directions, but realize that one way is faster. The possibility of exhausting your ammunition during a multiple-hostile engagement is a real concern. Study Chapter 10 ("Loading and Maintaining Continuity of Fire") and load what you shoot. Firepower is not a solution to a tactical problem, but it is comforting to have a few extra rounds of buckshot ready just in case.

Shooting several targets in succession is not difficult. The interval between shots is called *dwell time*. Dwell time occurs between the point that the first shot is fired and the point where the shotgun is realigned on target after recoil dissipates. This dwell time varies depending on the skill of the shooter, but it lies somewhere between 1/6 to 1/3 of a second. You can learn to use this dwell time to not only pump the action (if using a pump shotgun), but also to travel from one target to the next. You must learn to move the muzzle toward the next target on the recoil so that when you've pumped the action and reacquired the sights, you will have already aligned the weapon on target.

Your eyes will be involved in picking up the flash sight picture as well as in checking the status of hostiles you've shot or are about to shoot. Targets standing close together, abreast, or staggered can be shot very quickly. You can visually pick up the first one and align the shotgun on it. As the shot is fired, your visual focus remains on the front sight as the shotgun moves slightly to the next target during the recoil. When you notice that you've arrived at the next target through your peripheral vision, you fire the shot.

If the targets are spread out, the problem is more difficult. You must still deal with the first target as you did before. Now as the shotgun rises in recoil and begins moving toward where you think that target is, your visual focus must precede your arrival on target slightly in order to guide your shotgun to the target. Your face does not leave the stock to go looking for targets. Rather, your eyes will precede your muzzle by a slight margin. When the shotgun catches up to the eyes, the eye verifies the type of sight picture required for that particular shot, and the target is history.

There is no easy answer to the multiple-adversary scenario. This is truly a difficult tactical problem that you would best handle with a team that has double the number of adversaries. The best course of action is to withdraw, if possible, and if they press the issue—pick them off singly or in pairs during your tactical escape. If escape is not a viable option for whatever reason, then place them on the defensive and attack immediately. You don't have to be taking incoming fire to realize you are under attack. Being alert is the best defense of all because if you see trouble coming, you can prepare for it. For example, if you suddenly look up from your jelly roll and java at the local Doughnut Delight and see a trio of terrorists pointing their illegal, bayonet-equipped assault rifles at you, you've already lost that fight, haven't you? On the other hand, if you see these same characters slithering up your walkway on a crisp winter night at 0'dark thirty . . . well, you've won that fight before any shots are ever fired.

CHAPTER SIXTEEN

THE SHOTGUN AFTER DARK

". . . and remember the night is for hunting, and forget not the day is for sleep."

—Rudyard Kipling,
The Law of the Jungle

A great percentage of urban gunfights occur at night or, more specifically, during hours of darkness. This fact has given rise to an entire industry devoted to fulfill the needs of the night fighter. Many of the products that are passed off as essential are in fact gadgets and toys with little more utility than a child's laser pistol. While there are a few items that will enhance the individual's night combat capabilities, it is the ability of the man rather than the advancement of his tools that wins the fight.

The main problem in reduced-light environments is

143

not being able to illuminate the sights, but rather not being able to locate and identify the target. If it is too dark to see your sights, it is also too dark to be sure of what you are shooting at without some sort of illumination such as a flashlight.

You will not generally be operating in complete darkness. Unless you are hunting an adversary in a dark and windowless warehouse or the closed attic of an office building, you will have varying degrees of ambient light. These gradient increments do not fit into nice, neat categories. I have nonetheless divided their discussion into such categories for the purpose of clarity in examining the peculiarities of varying light levels.

The brightest low-light level is dusk. This light level occurs naturally from before sunset to about one-half hour afterward. A similar light level occurs at night in large, illuminated urban areas. This level of light allows you to distinguish your surroundings as well as those around you. Your sights are still visible, even if not as visible as at high noon. Shooting is no different at dusk than at any other time. Target identification is not an issue.

As the light continues to fade and the level of darkness increases, you will still be able to see your surroundings and distinguish persons in the area, but they are now backlit or silhouetted by the fading light still visible in the sky. Your sights are no longer as visible as before, and they now will seem to disappear when they are superimposed on a target. You will know where the sights are, and you'll still be able to verify a rough sight picture, but your reliance on programmed muscle memory to index the weapon on target will have increased. Anything beyond close-quarters shooting will be very difficult.

This is the light level where the popular radio-active tritium sights are at their best. When you shoulder a shotgun thus equipped, you will see the glowing element of the front sight instead of a fuzzy, dark blur.

When the level of remaining ambient light diminishes further, it will become very difficult to locate or identify any targets. You can still see your surroundings, but persons in the area are seen as indistinct shadows that seemingly blend into the dark background. Your sights are invisible at this point, and you must resort to artificial light. A flashlight works well for identification and illumination. Notice that while the presence of tritium night sights will not hamper the mission at this point, they will not assist in identifying or locating anything. What you need is some sort of flashlight to use in conjunction with the weapon. When you illuminate a target with a flashlight, your sights—tritium-equipped or not—will be silhouetted and appear as black sights against an illuminated background.

Any further decrease in the small level of ambient light places you in the realm of complete darkness. In complete darkness you will not be able to see anything. There will be no visual input at all in complete darkness. You cannot see the hostile, but you might be able to hear him. You can listen for sounds of breathing, footsteps, gunhandling, or any other noise that might be man-made. These sounds are target indicators, and they tell us that someone is nearby. By listening for these target indicators, you can index your light and gun to the source of that sound.

It is a human reflex to turn and look at the source of a sound. You train diligently to coordinate the gun muzzle with whatever it is the eyes are scanning, don't you? Eyes, muzzle, and target in line. Everything remains the same in the dark except that you don't have a target. You do have a sound that might indicate a target. Now you think eyes, muzzle, sound, and possibly target in line. This is the three-eye principle at its best. The muzzle is the third eye, and it looks at whatever the other two eyes are looking at. If you lock in on a sound, you might also lock in on the target. Since you are operating in darkness,

145

you must still identify such possible targets with artificial light to determine whether any shots are called for.

Your other senses will also serve you well in the dark. Olfactory target indicators for example are body odor, cigarette smoke, and cologne as well as other more primal scents given off by a human under stress. You may actually be able to smell the adversary's location without resorting to any light at all.

These light levels may be mitigated by varying degrees of ambient light, particularly in urban settings, where you may go from high noon to complete darkness by entering a building.

If there is enough light to see and identify a threat, any sighting aids or artificial lights are inconsequential. If there is not enough light to clearly see the sights but the targets are visible as backlit shadows, the night sights will allow you to index the weapon, but you still require target identification before shooting. When the background blends in with the possible targets as well as your sights, flashlights are mandatory and any other sighting enhancements are moot. A point that must be made here is that a flashlight is not intended as an aid to sighting, but rather as an aid to identifying a possible threat. You still need to aim.

There are relatively few effective methods of combining a shotgun with a flashlight. This problem is compounded when you attempt to combine a flashlight with a slide-action shotgun. But where there is a will . . . well, you know. The primary objective is to establish a coaxial balance between the light beam and the axis of the bore. You don't just want to locate and identify a possible threat, you want the capability to shoot him the instant you see him. Remember that you do not "snap shoot" into a flashlight position. Going into a tactical problem in the dark should give you a clue that you might need to bring a flashlight into the problem, no? If you perceive an immediate threat, you will deal with it as if it were daylight without resorting to a flashlight. If there was enough light for you to recognize a threat, there was enough light to handle it outright with standard means, otherwise you would not have seen it in the first place. You will probably be using a flashlight technique to look into a dark corner or maybe even to search an entire yard or building. The thing to remember is that there will usually be ample time to get into the flashlight position.

The best way to bring light into a dark tactical situation is simply to have it attached to the gun. My personal Smith & Wesson 3000 shotgun has a Laser Products Sure-Fire dedicated fore-end tactical light in place of the factory fore-end. A momentary switch allows my support hand to activate the light. The shooting position is the same regardless of the lighting conditions. You are never without your light as long as you have your shotgun with you.

A second way to incorporate the flashlight with the shotgun involves gripping both the light and the fore-end in the support hand. You must use a relatively small-diameter light unless you are built like Sasquatch. A C-cell flashlight can be held with the thumb and index finger in a sort of OK sign alongside the fore-end, and its on-off switch can be operated by the support-side thumb.

Most tactical shotguns are equipped with "white light" systems.

147

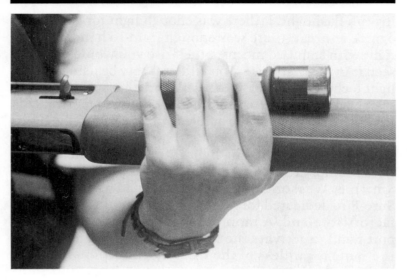

An alternate method is to grip a mini flashlight alongside the fore-end of the shotgun.

Although this works fine, a better option is to obtain one of the Laser Products Sure-Fire series flashlights or one of the Streamlight Mini Lights. These have both an on-off button on the side and on the end cap. The Sure-Fire has a twist-on end cap as well. If the end cap switch on the Sure-Fire light is turned to a point just short of turning the light on, any sideways pressure on the end cap will light things up. You can hold this light against the fore-end of the shotgun using a standard grip on the fore-end. The gripping pressure from your hand on the fore-end and flashlight body will now turn on the light.

You do not use a flashlight in a tactical situation by just turning it on and strolling through. You must avoid using it until it is absolutely necessary. You know that noise is a target indicator, right? Well, so is light if it is misused. A beam of light moving in the adversary's direction tells him you are looking for him. Also be careful about accidentally turning the light on with unintended grip pressure. A white-light "accidental discharge" will give you away as surely as if you'd fired a round into the ceiling. Know that as soon as your light goes on, your night vision is history, and it will not return fully for many minutes (a complete loss of night vision takes approximately 30 minutes to recoup). One possible solution to this that I've been experimenting with is to close your dominant (master) eye while lighting things up.

When you are scanning an area with light, do it from cover if possible. Sweep the light around the area that you wish to inspect for no more than a couple of seconds, all the time scanning for hostiles and remaining ready to shoot. Now, turn it off, and move quietly to a different vantage point and repeat this as needed to finish the mission.

Stay low and beam the light upward into the room. The light will tend to bounce off the ceiling and walls and wash the entire room with light. If you are working with a partner, he can light up the room in this fashion, while you stay under and outside the light beam. You will be invisible to anyone at whom the light is pointed. If the light is actually pointing at the adversary's location, he will either emerge from his hiding place to fight or remain presumably undiscovered, hoping that you'll overlook him. If he chooses to fight, the man with the light will shoot him. If he remains hidden, he will likely stay there while the light is on. You can now search in stealth and deal with him from a position of advantage when you see him. Oh yes, having a partner along to light things up for you while you search and to cover your back is a good idea, so add one to your equipment list whenever you go looking for things that go bump in the night!

CHAPTER SEVENTEEN

TACTICAL USE OF COVER AND CONCEALMENT

"From inside fortifications, the gun has no equal among weapons."

—Miyamoto Musashi,
The Book of Five Rings

*C*over. The very word invokes images of embattled police officers huddled behind something solid as a hailstorm of hostile gunfire crackles around them. In reality, cover is one of those essential elements, often ignored in training, that will help you emerge from a gunfight without any new holes.

The only problem with the use of cover is that you often don't have time to get behind it before the party starts. The vast majority of urban gunfights involve reactive situations where an individual must instantly *respond* to an unexpected act of hostility by

151

another. Additionally, these events often occur within spitting distance. If you recall the discussion of reaction times, you will remember that he who acts first will often win, particularly if he takes the other guy by surprise. You can usually minimize the surprise factor by maintaining an alert mind-set. But you must still contend with the social fact that you cannot generally conduct a pre-emptive strike on those who you suspect are about to attack. You must *react* to them. If you are allowed one reaction (all you will probably have time for at urban fighting distance), your best option is to counterattack immediately.

Allowing for the possibility that your alertness is heightened (as evidenced by the actual presence of a shotgun in your hands), you must still come to terms with the fact that you may not have the time, room, or warning to hide and must sort things out—right there in the open.

If you anticipate the threat and have the time to plan your tactics prior to the confrontation, you will also have the option of creating a respectable degree of distance from the hostile. This means that you should also get behind cover *before* the fight begins. Most of all, you must anticipate contact in order to realize the need to create distance from the source of the threat, which, in turn, will give you more time to get behind cover. Time, distance, and anticipation of danger are all intertwined. If you have these three things, you can use the option of cover almost at your leisure.

Even if the initial exchange of gunfire takes place in the open, don't think that you must stay there. As soon as you have control of the situation (however briefly, through your gunfire), you can begin to seek cover.

I am a firm advocate of moving away from the original firing location immediately. If you cannot move as you fire the first shot, you should certainly do so after the initial exchange. Your move should be toward cover. That act must be practiced as part of your daily training routine in order to make the entire idea and physical execution of seeking cover into a reflexive act, just as returning fire. Mount, shoot, sidestep to cover, keep the muzzle on the threat. Realize that I am not advocating sprinting to cover while you shoot. You need immediate termination of the threat with gunfire. This will deny your adversaries the time to shoot at you. But such a plan requires *hitting* them, which won't occur if you fire indiscriminately on the run. Movement to cover during firing means a controlled side step or two during your initial shots, followed by a controlled move away afterward.

Another situation where cover is of great importance is during any nonfiring operation such as reloading or clearing a stoppage. Make the cover option part of the immediate action drill so that when you realize the need to execute one of these operations, you will reflexively get behind cover as well.

Consciousness of cover is a part of being in Condition Yellow. Make it a mental habit to look around you periodically during the day and locate the nearest object that might serve as cover. Think about solid objects that you think would stop bullets or at least deflect them, such as big trees, brick walls, concrete blocks, vehicle engine blocks, metal lamp posts, and even fire hydrants.

Some items cannot provide any degree of ballistic protection at all and are merely concealment. The difference between the two is that cover provides varying degrees of protection from gunfire, whereas concealment only allows us to hide.

Don't dismiss concealment as a tactical option, because if your adversary doesn't know where you are, he probably won't be able to hit you. If he doesn't know you are there, the notion of shooting at you won't even enter his mind. Concealment demands silence, stillness, and stealth.

While cover can provide both a place to hide and protection from gunfire, concealment only allows you to deceive the adversary. Cover may be used before and during the fight. Concealment can only be used before the initial confrontation to either remain undetected or launch an unannounced attack of your own.

It is important to know the ballistic capability of various weapons in order to select suitable items to hide behind. If the adversary is armed with more powerful weapons, such as a centerfire rifle, there won't be many options for use as cover. For example, a cinderblock wall may be sufficient cover against pistol bullets or buckshot, but a .308 will sail right through it. Additionally, it is also good to know your own ballistic capability to be able to deal with your adversary's choice of cover. Vehicles, for example, are often involved in urban shooting situations, but only some parts of them are bullet resistant. The most resistant of these are the engine compartment and the metal wheels. Projectiles of varying ballistic capabilities will penetrate many parts of an automobile if fired at a perpendicular angle to its surface. As this angle increases, the penetrative capability diminishes, but ricochets increase.

These ricochets will generally travel parallel to the surface that they've hit and a few inches away from it. If you've assumed the "Hollywood hero" cover position (you know, the one where you drape your upper body over the hood of the car, with your arms extended over the other side), the ricocheting rounds will skip right into your scowling mug! Therefore, don't crowd the cover. Keep several feet back from it so that any ricochets will sail *over* you and not *into* you. Know also that you may use the same ricochet phenomena to skip pellets off any hard surface and into your adversary, in effect bypassing his cover. Don't worry about using any so-called barricade positions to steady your shooting unless the adversary is more than 100 yards away: keep back from cover.

When you shoot from behind cover, the best way is

154

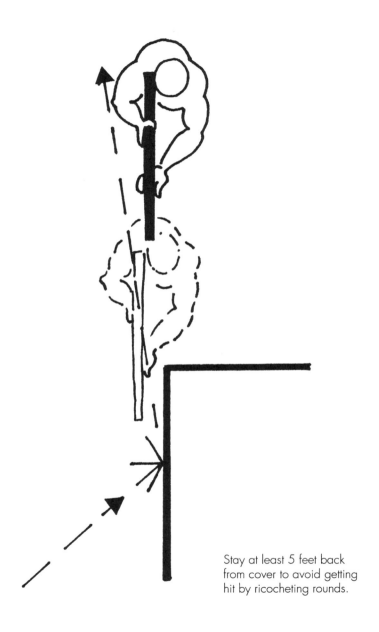

Stay at least 5 feet back from cover to avoid getting hit by ricocheting rounds.

155

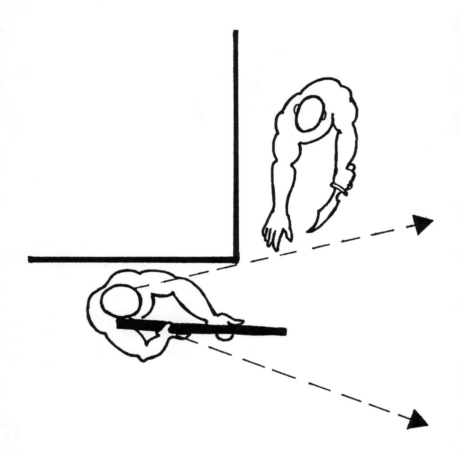

Do not let your
muzzle protrude
into unsecured
spaces for obvious
reasons.

to keep your weapon in a firing position and roll out just enough to clear the cover for your shot(s). You must allow the muzzle to precede you into the shooting position and withdraw the same way. Try to shoot around the cover instead of from above as this *may* minimize ricochets as well as expose less of you while you return fire. Do not allow the muzzle to protrude beyond your cover as this may present a weapon-retention problem. Avoid shooting from the support side unless you are wounded. Yes, you might present a slightly smaller target, but you will not be able to shoot as accurately. Remember, the purpose of shooting is to hit. If you are under fire, once you've reached cover, stay there. The only time it is advisable to leave cover is to prevent a flanking maneuver by an adversary. This means that if he is attempting to move to a location from which he can bypass your cover to shoot at you (and you cannot prevent this with gunfire), you must eventually evacuate your location to a new position of cover. A second reason to emerge from cover is to press your own assault or to attempt the same flanking tactic against our adversary.

Being able to anticipate danger is a product of an alert mind. This, in turn, is a product of a properly organized mind-set. In the not-so-ancient past, the penalty for being surprised while under arms was death. Today, in our "kinder and gentler" society, nothing has changed. The idea is to know that there is going to be a fight before it starts. If you are prepared for hostilities, you can dictate the course of the fight and eventually its outcome.

CHAPTER EIGHTEEN

SHOOTING WHILE MOVING (AND WHY)

"In my strategy the footwork doesn't change. I always walk as I usually do in the street."
—Miyamoto Musashi,
The Book of Five Rings

When you reach advanced levels, it is important to incorporate movement into the shooting process. This may be as simple as a side step when the shotgun is brought on target or as complicated as a complete flanking maneuver as required by the unfolding complexities of the events. Specifically excluded in this concept is shooting on the run. This will rarely be a realistic option, and even when it might be, its success will come more from luck than design. By movement I mean controlled travelling from one point to another while retaining the ability to

159

An operator may need the skill to shoot while moving from one location to another.

shoot and hit an adversary. Move only as fast as you can guarantee hitting your adversary.

If a gunfight is still in business after the first reactive shots are fired, you will want to evacuate your present location, which might very well be in the open. The reason for this is that the people whom you've had a disagreement with will initially be shooting at your original location. You might need to execute a quick side step as you fire again to solve the problem.

These close-quarters emergency side steps do not hinder your shooting speed or accuracy within arm's reach out to about 5 yards. Starting in a low-ready position, the emergency side step occurs as follows.

160

The underarm assault position is valuable for moving through a very close-quarters environment.

Movement to the dominant side begins with a quick shoulder-width step to the dominant side with the dominant (or trailing) foot. The support-side foot immediately follows with a similar step to reacquire the original stance about 3 feet from the original spot. Movement to the support side is similar in concept. The support (or leading) foot steps out to the support side with a shoulder-width step, and the dominant foot catches up, reestablishing the shooting stance to the left of the original spot. This same concept is useful for a quick step back. Using the rear foot, step back sharply and then catch up with the front foot.

These emergency steps might buy you an extra second or two in order to fire a second shot or cause your adversary to miss you with his own misdirected shot. By no means do you execute one single step and let it go at that. Keep moving with as many steps to the rear and sides as you need to solve the problem unscathed.

Many times an aggressor will choose to assault a victim when he is either turned away or profiled and presumably not paying attention. The concept of the emergency side step can be used to respond to the threats that appear to either side as well as to the rear. Proceeding from a low-ready position, I will explain the process for responding to threats to the right, left, and rear.

161

Response to a threat on the right side.

Response to a threat on the left side.

Facing forward in a low-ready position, you realize there is a hostile to the right. Pivot on the toe of the support foot and on the heel of the dominant foot. Simultaneously, bring the shotgun muzzle around to the dominant side and, pushing off with the support-side foot, step forward. This will reestablish your shooting stance and bring you on target.

Facing forward again, you realize a threat to the left side. Step forward with the dominant-side foot. Begin to pivot toward the support side (left) by pushing off with the dominant-side foot and bring the muzzle on target.

Dealing with a threat to the rear involves stepping forward and across the support-side foot. From this position, you simply pivot 180 degrees, or until you are facing in the opposite direction. It is a simple matter to bring the shotgun up to shoot as you complete the pivot.

These techniques may be used by a stationary operator or in conjunction with a subsequent side step. They may also be used to respond to threats while moving (in a ready-to-shoot mode), searching an area, or conducting a tactical entry.

A different type of moving and shooting might occur while moving through a hostile-held area to rescue a hostage, conducting a somewhat hurried search, or during a tactical team operation. In these situations it is important not to lose your forward momentum. The ability to attack the adversary and take him under fire while advancing has an overwhelming effect that may give you the necessary advantage.

The main consideration here is to alter the standard shooting position as little as possible while moving. The upper body from the waist up must become a gun turret that is minimally affected by the movement of the lower body. When you move, do so with the shotgun mounted in the shoulder and the muzzle lowered enough to be able to see any danger areas in front, but not necessarily pointing at the deck. The waist must be able to rotate

164

Response to a threat from the rear.

Shooting on the move is simply a matter of keeping the muzzle from "bouncing" as you walk.

left and right sufficiently for you to be able to cover danger areas as they are reached. The actual walking gait must differ as little as possible from your daily walking gait. The only modifications required are bending your knees to achieve a slightly lower center of gravity and leaning slightly forward to absorb recoil. The stepping involves a rolling heel-to-toe stride whether moving forward or to the rear.

Again, do not walk any faster than you can guarantee hitting your target. This usually means a brisk walking pace (neither a leisurely stroll nor a fast jog). Try to minimize any vertical motion of the weapon during movement. One field-expedient training exercise is to place a quarter on top of any flat portion of the weapon, such as the top of the receiver, and then proceed to walk up and down the range. The object of the exercise is to minimize vertical movement of the weapon as will be illustrated the first time your coin falls off the top of your gun.

The visual focus will be downrange, looking for a target to shoot. As soon as one is located, resist the urge to stop, raise the muzzle, switch visual focus to the front sight, and shoot. This will take considerably less time than it took to describe it here. The best practice method to enhance moving and shooting skills is the steel knockdown target. Set up pairs of them 2 meters apart and in two rows down the length of the range with about 5 meters between each pair of targets. The targets should be set up so that you can walk between the two rows on your way downrange. Now simply walk forward, engaging the targets to the left and the right. As this becomes easier, you can replace some targets with items of cover that you can move to, shoot from, and emerge from to engage again. Also, you can conduct this drill moving forward or to the rear.

Shooting on a parallel or diagonal approach is slightly different. The characteristics of a long gun (shotgun, tactical rifle, or submachine gun) will not allow you to use waist rotation as an advantage to engage these lateral targets as you could with a pistol. Additionally, I do not think that switching to the opposite shoulder midstride is a realistic proposition. When engaging such targets you must keep the shotgun in the same position it was on the approach and simply strive to face the targets during any shooting. The best way to accomplish this is to use a side step similar to the emergency side step. Multiple side steps become a sort of sideways shuffle similar to that used by a professional boxer. As you are walking forward with the weapon mounted in the shoulder, you notice a target appearing to the dominant side. As you approach the target, your support-side foot will step across the line of travel, and your rolling gait will become a sideways shuffle as the dominant foot catches up.

Moving laterally as you shoot is easily
accomplished, regardless of the
shoulder you shoot from (right or left).

Moving toward a specific objective that contains a threat may be accomplished with the forward shuffle step. Notice that the muzzle is pointed at the threat.

Shooting to the dominant side is not as difficult and involves simply rotating the waist to bring the weapon onto the target. The actual gait can be the original rolling gait or the sideways shuffle.

You can practice this technique by placing five targets abreast and about 2 meters apart at a 7-meter distance. Now simply practice moving from one end of the range to the other at the 7-meter line while engaging the targets.

If you are approaching a tactical obstacle during a search that may contain an adversary, you should slow down your approach considerably and transfer from a rolling gait to a forward shuffle. This forward shuffle becomes slow and deliberate as you approach the last few feet toward the possible confrontation.

The forward shuffle was developed by Chuck Taylor. It involves a forward step with the lead or support-side foot, followed by a catch-up step with the rear or dominant-side foot. The feet do not drag or scrape on the deck. This step is similar to how you would walk through a particularly narrow hallway that will not accommodate the width your shoulders. The shuffle step allows for a controlled and stealthy approach, providing you an opportunity to respond from a stable position if you are caught midstride.

Practice these movement drills forward, backward, and sideways. Drill them slowly with unloaded weapons at first and only venture to the firing range when you are completely comfortable with them.

CHAPTER NINETEEN

CLOSE QUARTERS WITH THE SHOTGUN

"Let the enemy come till he's almost close enough to touch, then let him have it and jump out and finish him up with your hatchet."

—Major Robert Rodgers
(founder of Rodgers Rangers),
Standing Order
Number Nineteen,
1759

An important concept in personal combat is to maximize your distance from the threat and to minimize your exposure to it. As we've discussed before, distance equals reaction time: the more distance from the threat that you have, the more time you have available to react. It is difficult to maintain this distance in a modern society, particularly in urban areas where many people live shoulder to shoulder. Additionally, even the best-laid tactical plans often go awry, and the shotgunner may find himself within arm's reach of Jack the Ripper.

171

The primary disadvantage of the shotgun in such close quarters is a lack of maneuverability because of its length. This is most evident when you try to search or move through a small house or a narrow alleyway, a task easily completed with a pistol. The shotgun's length makes it ungainly and cumbersome, sometimes causing it to bump against walls and protrude into unsecured space, or causing the operator to carry it in a less than advantageous manner (i.e., muzzle up toward the sky or muzzle down toward the deck). Often such situations also create weapon-retention problems.

Don't allow your muzzle to precede you into unsecured space.

The nature of close-quarters combat indicates that most confrontations occur well within the typical 7 yards that we often associate with urban gunfights. In fact, although 85 percent of these gunfights do occur within 7 yards, over half of those occur within the handshake distances of 5 feet. At 5 feet even a blind man with a rusty Raven .25 automatic can get lucky. The average man's reaction time is about 1/4 second—that is 1/4 of a second to *realize* that a fight is happening. When you add the time required to execute a rehearsed motor skill, the time increases to about 2 seconds. What can a blind man with a rusty Raven .25 auto do at 5 feet in 2 seconds? I don't know, but it will take you a couple of seconds to find out.

This brings us to an irrefutable truth about close

combat. Whoever moves first in a close-range gunfight usually wins. This discounts the Murphy factor of mindset and missed shots, but the proactive party will always be quicker than the reactive party.

The lesson is clear: move first! As Jeff Cooper says, "Be offsides on the play. No referee will call it back." To illustrate this point, try the following drills.

Secure one training partner and two flashlights (the ones with a push-button on-off switch). Face each other at a distances of 5 to 20 feet. Have your training partner initiate the drill by trying to illuminate you with his light in one quick motion as if the light were a firearm. When you see him move (or think that he is about to move), try to pre-empt his light by lighting him up first. You will find that your reactions are about 1/4 to 1/2 second behind his actions—and remember, you were *expecting* him to move.

Try a second drill actually involving shooting. Stand about 5 feet away from him as you both face downrange at two pepper poppers 7 yards away. Allow him to initiate the drill by shouldering his shotgun and shooting his popper. When you see him move in your peripheral vision (or think that he is going to move), shoulder your shotgun and knock down your target. Who hit his target first? Unless your partner is a sloppy shot and missed, his target fell first. Yours probably went down 1/4 to 1/2 second later. Get the picture? If you cannot get distance, and you cannot get behind cover, stop his attack with your own preventive counterattack. Move first!

When an adversary decides to shoot at you in a close-quarters situation, he won't be able to dally by waiting for a perfect sight picture as he aligns his weapon. If he does, you will kill him while he is getting ready. He will likely bring his weapon out and forward in a ballistic motion toward you (he might even be a—gasp!—point shooter). If you both stay where you are, you will both be shot by the other party, albeit one will get shot before the other.

173

Although you certainly cannot dodge bullets, you can dodge the direction of a weapon's presentation and the subsequent line of fire. Doing this may create enough lateral distance to keep you woundfree. In close quarters it is critical to move as you shoot and after you shoot. Ideally, after the first exchange, you will move to a covered position. This is not a complicated movement; it involves the emergency side step discussed in Chapter 18.

Does one side have an advantage over the other? Well, maybe. Stepping to either side is much preferable to simply standing there, but it is even better to step to the adversary's dominant side. You do this to

An adversary may launch an attack from the side.

stay to the back of his gun hand. You see, it is much easier for him to track you by redirecting his presentation toward his support side than to his dominant side. If you move to his dominant side and stay to the back of his gun hand, it may get you the slight edge needed to flatten him. You'll know which is his strong hand when he reaches for his weapon.

At 5 to 15 feet, the shotgun should be held in a position that favors weapon retention, such as in the underarm assault position. This will help prevent criminals from grabbing your gun, and it will enhance your visibility of close-range danger areas during searches.

At extreme close quarters, you may need to shoot at muzzle-contact distances. The destruction of tissue from a contact shotgun wound will be severe and extensive, and it is exacerbated by expanding and burning gasses that become part of the picture as well as shot-

Use the underarm position, or the indoor low ready, to negotiate the corner properly.

175

buffer material present in the shotshell. You should know that flesh and blood will often be ejected from the entrance wound because of the massive force created. This ejected meat will sometimes gum up the works of a firearm that has been fired in contact with the body. This is less likely if the recipient is shot on a clothed part of the body because the clothing will generally retain any ejected matter.

At spitball distances, weapon retention is an important issue, particularly with shotguns. You must realize that weapon retention is not a technical issue; it is a mental issue. This problem is best solved with an alert countenance and a proper mind-set. As the fighter pilots say, "check your six." The primary thing to remember is to keep the weapon as far from an adversary or a danger area as your tactics will allow.

You must realize that in most situations where a weapon is taken away from an operator, it will be used against him by the person taking it. Therefore, if someone tries to relieve you of your shotgun, you are quite justified in taking it hard—hard enough to use the deadliest force you can muster to keep them from taking it! Believe me, this is no time for control holds or verbal pleas. If you hurt them sufficiently, they will forget about your weapon. (Make the enemy worry about his own flanks, no?)

One notable U.S. Border Patrol officer, who has faced more than his share of elephants, relates an incident where a goon grabbed the muzzle of his shotgun for a disarm. The patrolman simply blew him off the end of the shotgun with a charge of 00 buck. Simple enough.

Step one is to do whatever you can to get the muzzle covering the would-be grabber. You can imagine what step two is. BOOM. If your shotgun is inoperative because of a malfunction or because it was grabbed before you had a chance to pump the action, then let him have it. That's right; let him take your inoperative shotgun (you know it

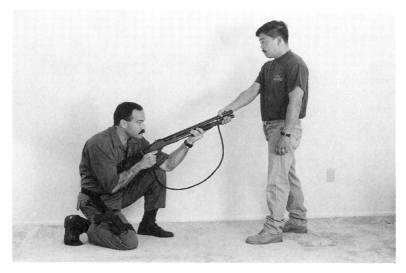

If an adversary grabs your muzzle, do not get into a tug of war. Get your muzzle pointed at him and blow him off the end of your gun.

177

If your adversary manages to get the upper hand by wresting the shotgun away from you before you can react, let him have it. Then let him have it with your pistol. After this, you may recover your shotgun from him. He won't want it anymore.

178

is inoperative because you just tried to blow his heart out with it and it didn't work), and after you obtain your pistol and shoot him, you can take it back.

Above all, when the fight has started, be violent! The more violent you become, the less aggressive your adversary will be. You can carry this up to the point dictated by your current rules of engagement.

Although it is generally discouraged, knowing how to use the shotgun as an impact weapon is a useful skill to add to your war bag. The shotgun has several useful striking areas. These are the muzzle for straight thrusts, the toe and heel of the stock for rising and horizontal strikes, and the bottom of the butt itself for short-range hard strikes. Additionally, the top of the receiver may be used for lateral thrusts.

Using the shotgun in such a fashion may be warranted if you are involved in a weapon-retention situation and the possibility of shooting your adversary is not an option because of a concentration of friendlies in the area or whatever. Also, if you are involved in a tactical team operation, you may encounter a semihostile who, while unarmed and not requiring gunfire, resists your orders to get down. Such people may even choose to get physical with you. A well-placed, alternate-force technique will usually elicit full compliance. Unconscious adversaries don't fight.

There are times when a shot will not only be justified, but also sorely needed. Yet many operators hesitate at the moment of truth because their background is too cluttered with uninvolved parties or friendlies. At such times you can assume a quick kneeling position or drop into a squatting position, thereby lowering the level of the gun mount and elevating its trajectory up into the adversary. Missed rounds or overpenetrating pellets will be travelling on an upward trajectory, and collateral injuries to bystanders will be minimized. This is a desperate tactic, but far better than standing there gawking

179

Alternate force may be used to subdue unarmed (nonshootable) adversaries. Here we see two versions of the muzzle thrust.

Depending on his distance from you, you may hit your adversary with the receiver or with the shotgun butt. Notice the body alignment behind the blow.

The shotgun butt may be used as a rising vertical blow, a horizontal blow, or a thrusting blow.

Sometimes you may need to move nonhostile resisters from your line of fire. Here are two methods of accomplishing this with escalating levels of violence.

while he punches your ticket! Yes, this may lead to law-suits. But while lawsuits are bad things, funerals are worse . . . especially if you are the guest of honor!

Consider also that there may be a situation where you've confronted a possible adversary at gunpoint, yet the circumstance did not call for gunfire or buttstrokes. What now? You must do three things in succession to maintain control of the scene.

1) Establish scene dominance.
2) Disarm the aggressor.
3) Secure the aggressor.

You establish scene dominance by taking a position from which to bring effective fire on an adversary without needlessly exposing yourself to incoming fire. This means that if you can, do use cover.

Because you are probably the one initiating the contact, you are in a position to dictate the circumstances of engagement (if he had initiated the confrontation with an attack, you'd have shot him, right?). This means that you can take a covered position before announcing your intentions.

It would be best to approach an adversary from behind, if possible, to lengthen his reaction time and maximize your distance, while still remaining close enough to be able to handle the problem.

Once you are behind cover and have your muzzle covering the target, you may issue a challenge. Remember that this is a nonshooting situation as far as you know. If he presents any threat, you will deal with him differently.

Another thing to bear in mind is that there is no guarantee that he will comply with your orders. He may just as easily produce his weapon and begin shooting when he realizes your presence. Even if he complies initially, he may have hopes of turning the tide of events, so be prepared to flatten him if he tries.

The shotgun muzzle is pointed at the subject in question but is lowered enough to be able to see him clearly, particularly his hands.

So just what do you say to the man under the gun? Talking and shooting are not compatible so keep your words short. Do not try to open up a discussion with this criminal. Not only might this distract you from the fact that this man is a *target*, but opening of negotiations may be seen as an exploitable weakness by him. His options are few: comply or die!

Avoid such vague and politically correct words as "appropriate action," which mean nothing to a criminal. Also, avoid gutter language words such as . . . well, just avoid gutter language. Also avoid empty threats that you do not intend to carry out. Strong, simple commands in conjunction with an attitude that conveys your willingness to kill will elicit more compliance than anything I know. Keep your words short and simple with hard consonants and few syllables. They must be forceful orders, not wimpy requests for compliance. Some good choices are *hold it, stop,* and *don't move.*

Do not order a movement at first. If you do, your adversary might feign compliance only to try to kill you while you stand around waiting for him to comply with your order. Remember action and reaction!

The next step is to disarm him if he has a weapon. If he has a gun in his belt, do not let him go near it. If he has a gun in his hands, and you have not shot him, I hope you had a very good reason. Order him to drop it at once. Allow it to hit the deck and stay there. Order him to step away from it and to turn his back to you. His hands should already have been placed in a reach-for-the-sky position.

The scene is now stable enough for you to secure your adversary. Order him to drop to his knees and then to get on the deck face down with his arms stretched out to the sides, palms up. He will find it very difficult to attack you from such a position. At this point, you may have your partner approach and secure him, or you may call for reinforcements. Exactly how you will do this must be planned beforehand, not at the scene.

Many confrontations will occur or develop at close-quarters distance. The perils of such engagements are much greater than those involving greater distances because of human reaction times when threats are within arm's reach as well as the rough marksmanship that will be sufficient to get hits (by either you or your adversary). With an understanding of these dynamics and a moderate degree of planning, you will be better prepared for any close encounter when armed with the shotgun.

CHAPTER TWENTY

SEARCHING TACTICS (INDOOR AND OUTDOOR)

"In planning, never a useless move. In strategy, no step taken in vain."

—Chen Hao,
Chinese scholar commenting
on Sun Tzu's *Art of War*

If you have the luxury of waiting, hidden and quiet, for your adversary to come to your fortified and covered location, and you are not forced to search for him in a structure, then you are quite fortunate. A home owner, for example, can simply ensconce himself behind his shotgun in the master bedroom, call the local authorities for reinforcements, and lie in wait for the intruder. Urban combat principles clearly indicate that built-up areas such as the interior of a building strongly favor the defender. Take every advantage if you hear an intruder or a home invader in the middle of the night.

187

But what if you are not sure exactly what that noise was in the living room? Was it the cat knocking over your wife's new vase, or was it something else? It is unlikely that you will spend the entire night in a barricaded fighting position, covering the kill zone that was once just a hallway, waiting for the Visigoths to mount their assault.

You and I would both probably go investigate the strange noise in order to dismiss it as harmless and go back to sleep. Similarly, a police officer who is detailed to conduct a building check will be in the same tactical position. In the officer's case it may vary from a simple check of an open door in the middle of the night to a full-bore tactical entry. Suffice it to say, there are times when you must go on the hunt, even if doing so is dangerous (it *always* is). It is hoped that the following words will help diminish that danger just a bit.

It is nearly impossible for a person to safely search an entire building single-handedly. There are occasions during such a search when you must turn your back on an unsecured area to check another one. This turns the search into a tactical coin toss: is the killer behind door number 1 or door number 2? A building search requires a team effort if it is going to be executed with minimal risk. This means that you must have someone to, at least, cover your back. When I search a building in which bad people are alleged to be hiding, I take two other men with me. One of them covers my back, while the other covers whatever area I am searching. Sometimes several of these three-man cells will be deployed to search a large structure.

You must understand that the geographic setting and architectural features that you encounter will dictate to some degree exactly how you conduct your search. Though there are no standard buildings, there are standard methods of movement within a building to minimize the danger to you while you search.

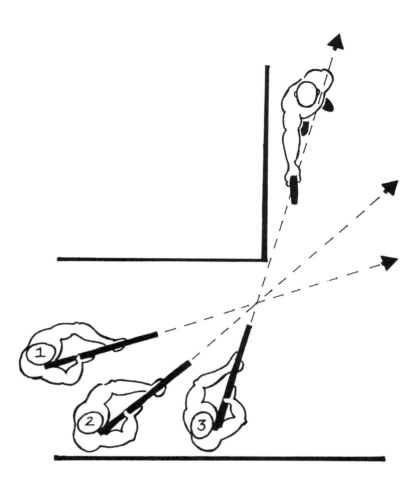

Clear corners slowly as if slicing a pie.

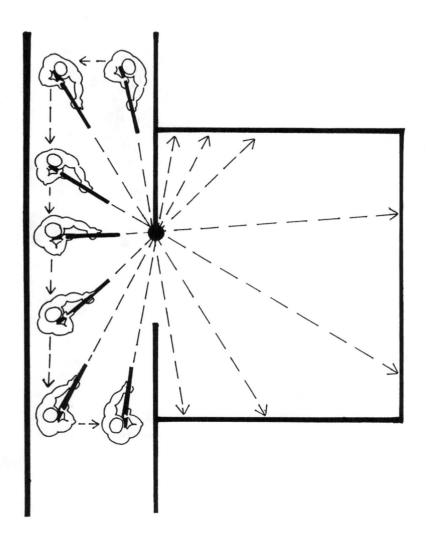

The same concept may be used to clear a room from the outside without actually making entry until the last moment.

What does this tell you about the corner you are about to search? What can you glean about the intentions of the person around the corner?

Think of an interior search as a series of angles, portals, and planes. A portal is a doorway, window, or any opening in the wall that leads into an unsecured area. The walls and the room within these portals are unsecured planes of space wherein an adversary may be concealed. The angles are your movement in and into these unsecured areas. A doorway, for example, is a portal that leads to the unsecured plane that is the room beyond it. Your approach to such a portal will rely on angular movement as you get near it. During a search you want to use angular movement to visually inspect as much of the unsecured spaces as you can before committing to enter. This technique is called "slicing the pie," and it is a modification of the concept of limited entry.

The first consideration is to use all of your senses such as sight, hearing, touch, and even smell to seek out target indicators. A target indicator is anything, however slight, that might indicate the presence of a hostile. Such target indicators include (but are not limited to) the sound of a footfall or the scraping of clothing as a person backs against the wall; the sight of the toe of a boot or a gun muzzle protruding from around a corner; a sniff of body odor, cigarette smoke, or even gun oil on a weapon. You simply have to pay attention to your senses and the information that they provide you.

You must also use your surroundings to your advantage. You may pick up reflections from any polished surface that may tell you what is in the next room. You can listen for a creak of floorboards and avoid them, and you can look through cracks in doors before entering them.

Never turn your back on anything you have not checked out and never assume that an area is clear unless you've seen all four walls as well as the floor and ceiling. Criminals will hide in the most unlikely places. You cannot shoot what you don't know is there, but what you don't know is there can certainly shoot you!

When searching with a team, each member must be assigned a specific area of responsibility and sector of fire as the team moves toward its objective. You must maintain your attention and ability to shoot at all times. Move behind your gun muzzle. Your maneuvering is designed to place your muzzle on any danger area and keep it there while it is being cleared. Keep your balance and stay under control physically at all times. Maintain the three-eye principle. Remember, this means that wherever your two God-given eyes look, your muzzle (the third eye) also looks, thus minimizing your reaction time considerably.

Stay away from corners and any architectural feature that may create a corner effect. Negotiate such features incrementally by "slicing the pie" until you have cleared the unsecured plane beyond it and you can see what is around the corner.

You handle a doorway the same as you do a corner in terms of "slicing the pie" from one side of the doorway. If the door is closed, you must determine which way it opens and place yourself in a position that will allow visibility into the unsecured space as soon as the door begins to open. If you can see the hinges, the door opens outward, and you should position yourself on the side by the door knob. If you cannot see the hinges, the door opens inward, and you should position yourself on the side across from the door knob.

Keep the shotgun close to your body when clearing or negotiating doorways or other small spaces. Do not linger in the doorway because if the hostile is in the room you are inspecting, all he needs to do is shoot toward the door to get you. Get through the doorway quickly after you've cut the angles as much as you can. When checking a room from the outside, be aware of slight discrepancies between the interior and the exterior. Going from a dark hallway into a lighted room is not bad. Going from a lighted hallway into a darkened room will immediately alert those inside the room because you will be backlit. A good option here would be to either light up the room or turn off the light in the hallway.

Visually search on a vertical axis (scanning up and down). Your visual scan should be in and out, moving the axis laterally every few feet. This is better than using a horizontal axis (a side-to-side search) because it gives your eyes a chance to view possible danger areas from several different angles. Remember that all you need to see is a target indicator, not the entire target.

Stairways present their own set of problems because not only do they channel your approach, but they also present vertical hazards as well as those normally associated with corners and hallways. Whether you search up or down depends on your location when you encounter the stairway. Whether one way is better than the other depends on the design of the stairway. Some stairways

193

have wells where a person approaching from above may be seen by those who are below through the spaces between the steps. This causes an operator to lead with his feet into a danger area instead of moving behind his muzzle. Be flexible with this and mold your tactics to the situation at hand.

The stairwell may be divided into the upper or lower landing and the steps themselves. You can clear the steps as you approach using standard techniques. To clear the landing, you must approach the now cleared steps and incrementally "slice the pie" until you've cleared what you can of the landing. Now is the difficult part when you begin the long climb or descent behind your gun until you reach the objective and clear that as well. Consider that there are often two or more sides to an upper landing and that you can only clear one of them at a time. Don't forget to bring a partner . . . or a coin to toss. Heads or tails?

There are also other features with which you should become familiar, such as hallways leading to rooms either directly or alongside. There are T-shaped hallways and L-shaped rooms. Consider all of these possibilities and practice dealing with them.

Don't be afraid to stop and simply listen to your surroundings, particularly if you've just made an accidental noise. Stop and listen for your adversary's reaction to it. Don't be afraid to trust your intuition about where the danger might be. This isn't ESP mumbo-jumbo; there are fleeting, subliminal clues that you may process subconsciously that send messages to your analytical mind about the events before you. These things are what we usually call hunches. For example, not long ago I was conducting an area search for a ding (a police term for a mentally disturbed person) with an ax who had tried to put the chop on a couple of taxpayers. While moving by one residence, I heard a slight metallic sound coming from the backyard. I paused and moved toward it after

194

Indoor shooting houses, such as this one, are invaluable for training.

signaling for my partner to follow. As we approached the rear gate of the yard and I was about to open it, I heard a clothes dryer in the backroom of the residence. It sounded like someone had forgotten to take the coins out of the pockets before laundering some pants. Something about the sound was different, but we rationalized that the sound of coins was what I'd actually heard. We bypassed that yard and went on to the next one. As we arrived at the next driveway, we saw our boy leap over the fence of the yard we had bypassed and run down the street away from us, ax in hand. Doom on us! He was captured moments later, but that didn't make up for our mistake. I won't let that happen again. Learn from my mistake and listen to that little voice; it may have something important to say.

When moving through open areas, walk briskly but quietly. When approaching danger areas, slow down and use the shuffle step. Clearing outdoor problems is no different, except that there is a degree of vastness not found indoors.

Single-handed clearing of a building is an exercise similar to Russian roulette. The more people you have with you, the less risk there is. But even with a three-man cell, it is still a risky business.

I hope the above information will be of help the next time you hear the goblins in the living room at 3 o'clock in the morning.

CHAPTER TWENTY-ONE

THE SHOTGUN IN SPECIAL OPERATIONS

"Go chase the red deer oe'r the heather. Run follow the fox if you can, but for pleasure and profit together . . . allow me the hunting of man."

—Rudyard Kipling, Requoted from *Gargantuan Gunsite Gossip* by Jeff Cooper

Although the submachine gun has all but replaced the shotgun in tactical circles, we shouldn't dismiss the smoothbore when talk turns to Nomex and flash bangs. Clearly, the shotgun is a much more specialized tool than the submachine gun for such activities, and it cannot be expected to fulfill the submachine gun's mission. Suitably modified, however, the tactical shotgun will serve with distinction in several spec-ops roles. Additionally, for many smaller agencies and teams, the shotgun is the only thing available. For those folks, the following suggestions might be beneficial.

197

The primary use of the SWAT shotgun today is for door breaching. A shotgun loaded with a frangible slug (intended specifically for shooting down doors) is used daily for breaching doors that for whatever reason are not rammable. Such shotguns are often equipped with a standoff device attached to the magazine tube, or a breacher device attached to the muzzle. A standoff device is a metal projection built up on the front of the magazine tube that keeps the muzzle off the surface of the door. This ensures that you do not damage the shotgun barrel through direct contact with the door. A breacher device is an actual part of the shotgun barrel that does the same thing but more efficiently. The primary purpose of a door breacher is to relieve muzzle gas pressure so that the muzzle may be placed in direct contact with the target without muzzle blowup. Breachers are available in titanium, steel, or aluminum and reduce about 80 percent of the muzzle-gas pressure created by firing a shotgun against a solid door.

The frangible slugs normally used for breaching purposes destroy the door lock and the surrounding door

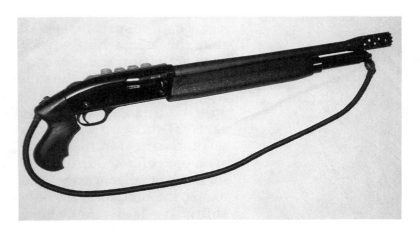

A special door-breaching shotgun used by a tactical unit.

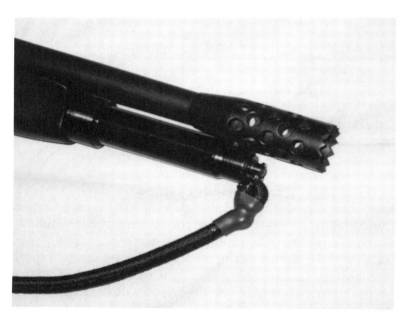

The business end of a breaching shotgun allows the operator to secure it in contact with the door surface, as well as dissipate the muzzle blast and prevent damage to the weapon.

A special breaching device for safely shooting off door locks.

without creating a hazard to persons within the room to be entered. The overall efficiency of a breaching round is measured by how well it defeats the door. Its degree of safety is measured by the efficiency of its frangibility. Additionally, if things do not go as planned, these breaching slugs will lose little in the stopping power department if they must be employed in an antipersonnel role within room combat distances.

Frangible breaching slugs can be fired point-blank from a suitably modified shotgun into the lock or hinge mechanisms of a door. As the round defeats these mechanisms, they disintegrate. Only fine powder may penetrate to the interior of the structure. Some teams prefer semiautomatic breaching shotguns to enable quick pairs in the event that one round fails to defeat the door. Additionally, since the weapon will only be used on doors, they do away with a buttstock and issue the piece with a pistol grip only.

The tactical shotgun in a snub-nosed configuration (14-inch barrel or less) is often found in the hands of a

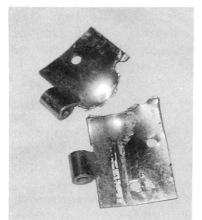

These fixtures were shot while attached to a door with frangible door-breaching slugs.

point man who is backed up by a submachine gun-equipped teammate. The reasoning behind this is that the pointman will cover probable danger areas while his more lightly armed associates actually do the searching.

Almost in complete contrast, other teams put the shotgun with the last person in line as a cover weapon (the tailgunner). This team member covers any danger area that has yet to be checked, or he may also be used to cover the 6 o'clock position. Additionally, in the event of an emergency extraction, the shotgun-armed tailgunner is the last man out and the last man firing.

Shotguns are also particularly useful for perimeter units and units conducting open-area searches with dogs. Although the submachine gun (as exemplified by the H&K MP5 or the Colt 9mm) is clearly the top choice for many tactical units, an issued shotgun in the hand is far better than an MP5 in the armory (or a Heckler & Koch catalog in the locker).

The question of the shotgun's role in hostage rescue comes up often. Using a shotgun to rescue hostages is somewhat like using a pipe wrench to hammer nails. It can be done, but the percentage of bent nails will be higher than if you used the proper tool in the first place. Either situation is not ideal and clearly should be avoided if possible. Sometimes, however, the pipe wrench will have to do because you've left the hammer at home.

Using the shotgun within the A Zone to quickly smash a hostile target who is partially hidden behind a "no shoot" hostage target is easy in the controlled confines of a shooting range. All you need are a basic understanding of the patterning characteristics of your shotgun and a quick shoulder mount. You fire as soon as the sights appear on the target and hold slightly off to the side opposite the hostage. This will "scallop" the bad guy with a half pattern and save the day.

It is different when the hostile human is not exposing himself and is growling at the top of his lungs that he'll kill the hostage as he presses the muzzle of his pistol under her chin. Meanwhile, the hostage will be screaming and crying, squirming and trying futile escape attempts. The hostile criminal will not let her go because he knows he is safe as long as she is in the way: he won't have to go back to prison, and you won't kill him as long as he has that hostage. But if you don't do something now, he might shoot her or begin to bring his muzzle to bear on you and kill you while you stand there deciding your options.

Not as easy as it was at the range, is it ? You will have milliseconds to decide what to do. Unless the hostage is about to have her throat cut in the next second if you do not act, a good choice is to withdraw and secure the scene to prevent the bad guy's escape. Even if you cannot contain him, you cannot leave him with the hostage (that usually means the later death of the hostage). Also, if the hostage is a family member of friend, you will definitely not want to allow an escape. You alone will have to solve the problem.

Attempting to solve a hostage problem with a shotgun is the least flexible of options. If you have a pistol handy, secure the shotgun and handle the situation with the handgun. If you must handle a hostage rescue with a shotgun, consider the following three things.

1. A thorough knowledge of the patterning characteristics of your shotgun and ammunition.
2. A Zone engagement to obtain the single projectile effect within 5 yards—the closer the better.
3. The confidence to seize the initiative and shoot without hesitation when the window of opportunity opens for you. It is also advisable to hold at the hostile's ear on the side opposite the hostage so that you can minimize any pellets striking the hostage. You only need to hit your target with one or two pellets to disrupt his position and, it is hoped, his grip on the hostage. Once the hostage is clear, shoot the hostile until he is flat.

If the hostage problem is farther away than the A Zone, either hold your fire or close the distance. There is no other option unless you can switch to a slug and guarantee sniperlike accuracy out of your gun.

Shotguns are developing into a more limited weapon in special ops. These scenarios are better solved with the pistol or submachine gun. Here the author and Chuck Taylor conduct a high-angle entry at the Front Sight Firearms Training Institute's Special Operations Course.

If you expect a hostage rescue problem and you only have a shotgun available to you, load it with slugs. Hostage rescue demands surgically precise shooting, and this is better accomplished with a service pistol or a tactical submachine gun. Purposely conducting a hostage rescue with a shotgun is ill-advised, especially if you have a pistol or an MP5 available.

CHAPTER TWENTY-TWO

ONE-HANDED OPERATION OF THE SHOTGUN

"You are only beaten when you admit it to yourself."

—Hans Ulrich Rudel,
Requoted from *Fireworks*
by Jeff Cooper

An old karate master once warned me not go into a fight thinking that I would come out uninjured. He believed correctly that if you accepted the very real possibility of your being injured it would not surprise you when it happened. His philosophy also included practicing techniques for when you had to fight in spite of such injuries.

You may easily expand this empty-hand concept and say that any man who has the possibility of being in a gunfight should consider the possibility of being shot. You must understand that only a minor percentage of the many

207

citizens who are shot every year on both sides of the law ever die, much less drop on the spot. This means that you should program the combat data center that is your mind that, if you are shot, you *will* shoot back. Program the attitude that if one arm is disabled, you will continue to fight with the other one.

Often the mere act of returning fire after you've been injured will be sufficient to save you (even if you do not kill your attacker). Other times, you will have to fight and win a small war one-handed as the shotgun-armed FBI agent did during the legendary Miami gunfight on

Shooting the shotgun one-handed in a firefight is not on the top of most people's Christmas lists.

April 11, 1986. On that date, two FBI agents stopped a dark Monte Carlo containing two men suspected of armed robbery and radioed for backup. This famous shootout, which lasted only about five minutes, resulted in the death of the two suspects as well as the deaths of two FBI agents and injuries to five others. But FBI Agent Ed Mireles, though wounded, still managed to operate his pump-action shotgun and shoot back, one-handed!

The biggest problem with one-handed operation is the actual weight of the shotgun. In times like these you will probably have enough reserves that the weight will not be an issue, but it might. If this is the case, responding from the underarm assault position might be a good option. Having one hand disabled makes tracking an opponent lat-

"Pumping" the action of a shotgun with one hand is performed by using gravity and momentum.

If the circumstances require that you keep shooting, and you are wounded, and your shotgun is empty, ditch the shotgun and shoot with your pistol.

erally especially difficult. To accomplish this, you must actually turn your entire body to index on the target.

There can be no denying that for one-handed operation the shooter of the semiautomatic leaves the slide-action miles behind. But if you are armed with a slide-action, the fight is not lost. Sometimes a well-worn or slicked-up action will unlock far enough on the recoil of a shot to allow a wounded operator to briskly jerk the gun to the rear butt first and then suddenly halt the motion of the shotgun. This will often extract and eject a spent shell. A similar motion forward will feed and chamber the next round. An alternate method for those with stiff actions is to grab the shotgun by the fore-end and, holding it muzzle up, jerk the gun upward. As the shotgun reaches its highest point, violently jerk the fore-end down and immediately back up. This will both

210

To reload the shotgun, place it between your knees and load into the magazine as usual.

extract and eject the spent shell, as well as feed and chamber the next round.

Though loading a shotgun one-handed in the middle of a firefight is not everyone's daydream, it is far better than surrendering. But consider again what I pointed out earlier: if you have a loaded pistol on your belt and an empty shotgun in your one functioning hand, and there is a Viking with an ax coming to part your thinning hair with a downward chop, what is your best option? If you said to ditch the shotgun and go for the pistol, then you get the cigar! Switch to a second weapon to solve an immediate threat immediately.

In spite of this you may still need to reload the shotgun one-handed. The best method to accomplish this is to clamp the shotgun between your knees, loading port up and muzzle forward. The action should be open (fore-

211

end or bolt to the rear). Load the first round into the ejection port and either run the fore-end forward or close the bolt. If you need to shoot right away, at this point you can. If not, then complete the loading of the shotgun through the loading port. All of these techniques may be accomplished while you are standing or lying flat on your back.

In the title page of this chapter I quoted perhaps the greatest warrior of our time—Hans Ulrich Rudel. His accomplishments have been written about by Jeff Cooper in his book *Fireworks*. Other than extreme personal skill, Rudel's most important asset was attitude. His story is there for anyone who cares to read it. He said (and meant every word), "A man is only defeated when he admits it to himself." Keep him and his words in mind if you ever have to shoot back after you've been wounded.

A FINAL WORD

Success in personal combat is a matter of attitude and equipment. Although it is true that any weapon will do if the operator is up to the task, good equipment enhances the warrior's ability to fight. A prehistoric stone ax will serve nicely in the proper hands and at the right moment, but a tactical shotgun would be much more effective. As yet, stone axes have not been banned, but, given time, the enemies of freedom may get to them as well.

Increasingly, we see forces within our nation that wish to do away with our martial effectiveness by taking away our

"The Modern Technique of the Shotgun" concept was first conceived by Jeff Cooper. He is seen here reviewing a class.

ability to fight. They want to protect us from ourselves and bring us into the kinder and gentler (read: softer and weaker) "Age of the Wimp." No thank you. Not for me! These well-meaning felon-huggers claim to side with the police against all that ails our society, yet no true police officer whom I've ever met sides with them or their cause.

A wise man once said that while times change, people do not. Any study of history would show the foolishness of a disarmed society as easily as it would show the evils of a totalitarian government. The two seem to go together. I would imagine that if any of these antigun types had ever lived under the Communist fist and experienced the evils of tyranny firsthand, as I have, they would instantly realize the idiocy of their philosophy . . . and go buy a gun.

I wish that these people would study history. If they did, they would learn that evil men have always been, and still are, a large part of the human experience. They would also learn that unless good men have the will and ability to resist them and fight them, their evil will triumph and spread. And, finally, they would learn that these evil men may be found lurking, not only in the back alleys of the urban jungles disguised as street terrorists who would steal our money, but also in the halls of government dressed as antigun legislators who would steal our freedom. It is every man's duty to be willing and able to protect himself and his family against these men and, by doing so, ensure his own freedom as well as that of his family—and, ultimately, that of his country. This includes voting appropriately.

We must fulfill our solemn duty to preserve the freedom that so many have died for. We must all join and support the NRA and become involved in the political process. We must make certain to elect only those who echo our concerns about preserving the American way of life—a way of life whose existence revolves around individual freedom and responsibility—a way of life that demands the private ownership, not of duck-hunting equipment, but rather of weapons . . . weapons such as the tactical shotgun.

SOURCES FOR EQUIPMENT AND TRAINING

Front Sight Firearms Training Institute
P.O. Box 2619
Aptos, CA 95003
The best place to receive training in the use of the shotgun

Laser Products
18300 Mt. Baldy Circle
Fountain Valley, CA 92708
Dedicated flashlight-tactical light fore-ends for shotguns

MD-Labs
856 S. Highway 89
Chino Valley, AZ 86323
Thermoplastic shotgun shell pouches and other gear

Royal Arms International
P.O. Box 6083
Woodland Hills, CA 91365-6083
Tactical Quick Sling as well as breaching shotguns and ammunition

Simmunitions, Inc.
366 Bruyere St.
Ottawa, ON
CANADA, K1N 5E7
FTX training ammunition

SUGGESTED READING

Awerbuck, Louis. *The Defensive Shotgun: Techniques and Tactics.* Cornville, AZ: SWAT Publications, 1989.

Cooper, Jeff. *Fireworks.* Paulden, AZ: Gunsite Press, 1990.

_____. *Principles of Personal Defense.* Paulden, AZ: Gunsite Press, 1979

_____. *To Ride, Shoot Straight, and Speak the Truth.* Paulden, AZ: Gunsite Press, 1988.

Garfield, Charles A. *Peak Performance.* New York: Warner Books, 1984.

La Pierre, Wayne. *Guns, Crime, and Freedom.* Washington, D.C.: Regnery Press, 1994.

Loehr, James E. *Mental Toughness Training for Life.* New York: Penguin Books, 1993.

Millman, Dan. *The Warrior Athlete*. Walpole, NH: Stillpoint, 1979.

Musashi, Miyamoto. *A Book of Five Rings*. Twinsburg, OH: Harris, 1974.

Plaxco, Michael. *Shooting from Within*. Zediker, 1991.

Suarez, Gabriel. *The Tactical Pistol: Advanced Gunfighting Concepts and Techniques*. Boulder, CO: Paladin Press, 1996.

Sun Tzu. *The Art of War*. Translated and edited by Samuel B. Griffith. New York: Oxford, 1963.

Taylor, Chuck. *The Combat Shotgun and Submachine Gun*. Boulder, CO: Paladin Press, 1985.

Remsberg, Charles. *Street Survival*. Northbrook, IL: Calibre Press, 1980.

The Tactical Edge. Northbrook, IL: Calibre Press, 1986.